DID SOMEBODY STEP ON A DUCK?

DID SOMEBODY Step ON A Duck?

A NATURAL HISTORY OF THE FART

Jim Dawson

TEN SPEED PRESS
Berkeley

Published in the United States by Ten Speed Press, an imprint of the Crown Publishing Group, a
division of Random House, Inc., New York.
www.crownpublishing.com
www.tenspeed.com

Ten Speed Press and the Ten Speed Press colophon are registered trademarks of Random House, Inc.

Lyrics to "Why Do Girls Think I'm Scary" reprinted on page 149 by permission of Da Yoopers
(www.dayoopers.com).

Library of Congress Cataloging-in-Publication Data

Dawson, Jim.
  Did somebody step on a duck? : a natural history of the fart / Jim Dawson. — 1st ed.
    p. cm.
  Includes bibliographical references and index.
  Summary: "A new collection of gas-passing anecdotes, popular culture references,
and historical tidbits from fart historian Jim Dawson"—Provided by publisher.
  1. Flatulence—Humor. I. Title.
  PN6231.F55D395 2010
  818'.602—dc22
                              2010000441

ISBN 978-1-58008-133-7

Printed in the United States of America

Design by Betsy Stromberg

10 9 8 7 6 5 4 3 2 1

First Edition

CONTENTS

ACKNOWLEDGMENTS

Thanks to M.K. Aldin, Monique Althaus, Holly S. Anderson, Katey Walter Anthony, Jon & Mary Bango, Lynne Bateson, Bob Birchard, Dick Blackburn, Leslie Blasco, Bob Board, Crai S. Bower, Denny Bruce, Edgar Bullington, Ray Campi, John Chambliss, Mike Chu, Joel Comm, Sol Cooperson, Mandy Covey, Dr. Trevor Cox, Sue Dadd, Jim DeCaire, Nancy Delfavero, Dr. Demento (Barrett Hansen), Todd Everett, Art Fein, Harvey Sid Fisher, Peter Ford, Alison Gallant, Bill Gardner, Stu Goldman, Libby Goold, Melrose Larry Green, Michael Gwynne, Kristi Hein, Skip Heller, Jill Hutchinson, Joan Kahn, Kate Karp, Larry Karp, Bill Kay, Tom Kenny, Paul Krassner, Steve and Jeanette Lamb, T.K. Lamey, Paul LaPann, Allen Larman, Johnny Legend, Arnie Leibovit, Bobb Lynes, Mabel Mackey, Ivor Masters, Dr. Paul McDonald, William Mitchell, the late Brendan Mullen, Harry Narunsky, Opal Nations, Michael Ochs, Guy Pohlman, Steve & Sylvia Propes, Ray & Maria Regalado, Earl Reinhalter, David Reskin, Jeff Riley, Glenn Robison, Will Ryan, Ed & Amy Schofield, Andy Schwartz, Gene Sculatti, Linda Somerville, Phil Spector, Gloria Stanford, Bruce Stockert, Larry & Janey Stonko, Dave Stuckey, Mark Tortoricci, Billy Vera, Barbara Watkins, Frank Weimann, Lisa Westmoreland, Ian & Regina Whitcomb, Jonny Whiteside, and Robert Yacko for helping me restore charm, elegance, and romance to the world of farting.

INTRODUCTION

Whoa, did somebody step on a duck?

—AL CERVIK (RODNEY DANGERFIELD), after letting a long,
wet one at a society dinner, in *Caddyshack* (1980)

A fart changes the atmosphere. In a 2007 *L.A. Weekly* review of a book about
theater mishaps, Steven Leigh Morris recalled a personal moment at a performance of Euripides' *Iphigenia.* During the murder of the heroine by her
father, "somebody in the audience of about one hundred people released a
very small, involuntary fart—an accident, not a commentary," Morris wrote.
"Cutting through the silence, it was audible through at least the front half
of the audience and by the actors—assorted guards and spear-carrier types
in particular—who were clearly reaching into the marrow of their bones to
contain giggles that were rolling through them in small, powerful waves."
Over the next few minutes, their "mirth suppression" hijacked the Greek
tragedy and "crossed the footlights into the house. Suspension of disbelief
unraveled. . . . The tiniest of farts had sent the walls crashing down."

In our public life we hold at bay a disbelief that is not all that different
from what we suspend at the theater. We know that when we're sitting at
home in front of the TV, we pick our noses, scratch our asses, and fart to
our hearts' content, but when we run down to the store for another six-pack
or a bag of chips, we wrap ourselves in a veil of propriety because we want
to be acceptable to all those other surreptitious farters hiding their true

selves from us. Essentially, we're denying our knowledge that we're nothing more than tricked-up mammals, a mere baby step up from chimps and orangutans, struggling to adhere to a social code our mothers drummed into us while we sat on the potty.

That's why the atmosphere changes—in more ways than one—when someone inadvertently lets a big one at the checkout counter or a small one in a quiet theater. A fart can instantly erase the luster from a beautiful girl—or make her touchingly vulnerable. It can strip the authority from the cop who's giving you a ticket or the priest presiding at communion. We're shocked, not because we didn't already believe everybody farted, but rather because someone (usually unwillingly) confronts us with the big lie that underpins our conformity to social norms.

When Ten Speed Press released *Who Cut the Cheese?* in 1999, a major columnist at the *Los Angeles Times* told me that no family newspaper, including his, would ever print the word *fart*. A few years later the *Times* broke that barrier by using the term *old farts* to describe fogeys who weren't keeping up with youth culture. And now the word pops up fairly often in its full flatulent context. In early March 2009, for example, columnist Meghan Daum lamented the loss of a Los Angeles talk-show station with "I'm taking my fart-joke business elsewhere." In a June 19, 2009, film review, *Times* critic Betsy Sharkey described the Jack Black/Michael Cera comedy *Year One* as a "turn-back-the-clock, take-a-look-at-our-ancestors fable with fart jokes." And on October 3, 2009, the *Times* Calendar section's front page broke the visual barrier by running a large, top-of-the-fold photo of children's comic-strip author Berkeley Breathed with several of his illustrated dogs, including one propelling itself through the air on a skateboard with a whooshing trail of chunky—and I do mean chunky—fart gas. Meanwhile, the *Chicago Sun-Times* has not only run several articles about the ubiquity of fart humor in American culture today, but also phoned such personages as professional farter Mr. Methane and even yours truly for a quote or two. Clearly, the age of the fart is upon us, and we can deny it no more.

In fact, as you'll see in these pages, farts are everywhere, in politics, science, religion, history, sports, entertainment, and . . . well, what's left? We even discover new ones every day, such as the *fargle*, which is a fart that doesn't quite escape as you lean forward to slip it out, and when you lean back too soon, it's forced back in and makes a reverse fart noise. Or how about the new *courtesy fart*, which is what you offer when someone else accidentally lets one go and you don't want them to feel like an outcast?

Okay, I know, you're asking yourself, what kind of smart feller (an old hillbilly jibe meaning *fart smeller*) who's well into middle age writes three books about farting? Obviously he's not well. As radio host Stephanie Miller told me ten years ago during my media blitz for *Who Cut the Cheese?* (the trilogy opener), "Jim, you're a very sick man, and you're spending way too much time by yourself." Another talk show host, Bill Handel, thought I should be locked up (though he did love the book).

I suppose I could blame this fixation on arrested development. But before anyone accuses me of having the sniggering sensibility and emotional maturity of a twelve-year-old, let me assure you right now that I've progressed to at least age seventeen, maybe eighteen. Granted, that's pretty much where I've stayed, but nobody's perfect. Nearly fifty years have passed since my high school graduation, yet my daily wardrobe is still sneakers, jeans, and T-shirts; my music of choice is 1950s rockabilly and rhythm and blues; my favorite movies are postwar films noir and zombie bloodfests; my romantic ideal is still the exotic, dark-eyed girl with a bouffant high enough to tangle with a ceiling fan; and nothing will get me giggling with dimwitted delight like a well-placed fart. (Oh, and did I mention, ladies, that I'm single?) Yes, I'm too old for this nonsense, but then again, if I were a mature adult I'd be retiring right about now from some cubicle confinement and suffering degenerative brain function (not that there's anything wrong with that), and you wouldn't have the pleasure of my company.

So enough with the fanfare. Let the gamy prose begin.

1

I FART, THEREFORE I AM

When I was in the Marines in the 1960s, I heard a lot of colorful oaths and aphorisms from grizzled lifers who had picked them up a decade or two earlier, during one of the wars. One memorable line, meant to be delivered when a beautiful but unobtainable girl walked by, was: "I'd lay ten miles of comm wire through thick jungle just to hear her fart over a field phone!"

It never crossed our minds that someday people would carry around little phones that actually farted—and that a guy named Comm would have something to do with it.

You can blame the cellular phone, which has probably had more impact on our daily lives and personal habits than any other invention since television. The cell phone has its own (lack of) etiquette, its own language, its own alphabet, even its own laws to regulate its use in common situations, like driving a car. But more significantly, over the past few years it has evolved into the "smartphone" and surpassed its original function by becoming an all-purpose computer—a palm-sized extension of the owner's nervous system. The product that dramatically sped up its insinuation into our daily lives was Apple's iPhone, a veritable electronic Swiss Army knife with WiFi internet access, which was in seventeen million hands within a year and a half after its June 2007 debut. *Time* magazine dubbed it the "Invention of the Year."

What gave the iPhone its edge was Apple's software development kit, available to all, democratically allowing any clever computer geek the chance to write his or her own application (mini-program) and sell it through Apple's iTunes' App Store. Before long, you could download an app onto your iPhone to satisfy nearly any impulse, no matter how whimsical. Among the tens of thousands available, there's a GPS app that tells you exactly where you are at any time and how you can find anywhere you want to go from there, be it the nearest French restaurant or the most pretentious French restaurant within fifty miles. There's even an app that turns your phone into an ocarina—an ancient Aztec flute—that you can play by blowing into the mouthpiece and fingering four note buttons on the screen.

But what really caught the world's attention was the iFart Mobile app, introduced on December 12, 2008—a date that will live in, well, infamy perhaps. Suddenly anyone, for just ninety-nine cents, could enjoy a good fart over the phone—not just one monochromic poot but a library of twenty-five different "pharts," including the Air Biscuit, the Honk, the Brown Mosquito, the Butt Socket, the Burrito Maximo, the Jack the Ripper, and the Silent-But-Deadly (first silence, then a disgusted voice moaning "Ohhhhh, *man!*"). You could turn any one of them into your iPhone's sputtering ringtone or email and text-message them to your friends and ex-spouses. Better yet, iFart let you record a real snort from your own fart funnel and send it to a loved one who, you hope, would recognize its distinctive loveliness the way a mother bird knows the chirps of her babies within the cacophony of a nesting colony. Or you could turn your very own fart into your *very* personal ringtone. There's also a time-delay fart (the "Sneak Attack") that functions like an electronic whoopee cushion (thus superseding the battery-powered Fart Machine that I spotlighted in *Blame It on the Dog*). The program even has a motion-detection alert ("Security"). Lay your iPhone down on a flat surface, and if someone picks it up, it farts—alarmingly!

The iFart was a hit from its day of release. It zoomed up the App Store chart to number one just before Christmas and lingered there for three weeks. The iFart's designer is Joel Comm, an Internet businessman who had already made a name for himself by cocreating Yahoo! Games and producing and hosting the first Internet reality show, *Next Internet Millionaire*. Comm noted on his blog (joelcomm.com) that during just two days alone—Christmas Eve and Christmas Day—his InfoMedia, Inc. sold more than 58,000 downloads, netting over $40,000 dollars. Said Comm, "iFart is a cultural phenomenon." By spring 2009 he had increased his arsenal of arse-squeak options to nearly one hundred. In July he bragged to the *San Francisco Chronicle* that his sales had passed the million mark to reach "flatulence superiority" over all the other farting apps.

Yes, there were dozens of others in iFart's wake, including Fart Button, Mr. Poot, iToot, iFartz, FartBox, Whoopee Cushion, Who Farted? and Pull My Finger, which presented a virtual index finger on the touch screen that produced a fart noise when "pulled." There was even a game with flatulent sounds called iLightFarts, challenging the player to burn them off as quickly as they happen or else be overwhelmed by gas. According to David Chartier in a February 2009 ArsTechnica.com blog post, "You may not believe it, but fart tools are among the largest categories of iPhone apps. In fact, outside of games—the most popular apps—fart apps may very well take the lead. A quick search for 'fart' in the App Store produced well over one hundred results."

But by mid-2009, fart fatigue was setting in. Alex Miro, whose Krapps .com covered the exponential growth of iPhone's apps, told the *Chronicle* in July, "Some of this stuff is funny, and I'm no prude, but where is Apple going with all this? It gets to the point, after the first ten farting apps, I stop writing about it. It's old and idiotic." Comedian Bill Maher concurred by coming up with one of his trademark New Rules: "If your phone can fart, you're part of the problem."

Clearly all this electronic flatulence was turning out to be too much of a good thing. When Joel Comm began using the phrase "pull my finger" in his iFart ads, he yanked the crank of Pull My Finger's creator, Eric Stratton of Air-o-Matic. Stratton threatened Comm with a lawsuit for trademark infringement and unfair business practices and wanted $50,000 to settle the dispute. The combustible Comm preempted him by filing a formal complaint in federal court asking for a declaratory judgment that "pull my finger" was a colloquialism that couldn't be trademarked. "The phrase 'pull my finger,' and derivations thereof, are generally known and widely understood in American society to be a joke or prank regarding flatulence," Comm said in his filing. "The prank begins when the prankster senses the deep stirrings of flatulence." (For a more detailed history of the pull-my-finger gag, see the "Fickle Finger of Farts" chapter in *Blame It on the Dog*.)

In February, FoxNews.com billed the brouhaha as an "iPhone Flatulence Fakers Feud" and noted, "It's a real stinky situation." Fox had its fingers crossed that "the case will go all the way to the Supreme Court, just so we can hear the nine highest jurists in the land read aloud passages such as . . . 'Butt Socket.'"

By April the methane-like flare-up was history. (Comm and Stratton would later take their case to *The Daily Show with Jon Stewart* and make up in a flurry of air kisses.) Public outrage had already moved elsewhere, thanks to iPhone's new "Baby Shaker" app that let the user shake a crying infant until its eyes changed from lively Os to brain-dead Xs. GottaBe Mobile.com summed up the outcry in an April 22 entry: "After things seemed to settle down from the obnoxious cloud of apps featuring . . . the sounds of flatulence, Apple seems to be once again approving apps that have questionable value and taste." Apple pulled Baby Shaker off the market after only two days. Suddenly the idea of making your phone fart like a young Marine after a night of sucking down pickled eggs with cheap beer seemed innocent and fun. So goes the demise of Western civilization.

2

---•

BUSH-LEAGUE BUTT BURPS

In mid-August 2006 *U.S. News & World Report* columnist Paul Bedard ran an innocent little item titled "Animal House in the West Wing" in which he claimed that George W. Bush was "a funny, earthy guy who, for example, can't get enough of fart jokes. He's also known to cut a few for laughs, especially when greeting new young aides, but forget about getting people to gas [complain] about that."

Coming from a respected conservative newsstand magazine, Bedard's revelation sent a mega-blast wave through Washington, even though it wasn't the first time news had leaked out that the "first frat boy" had a penchant for poot pranks. Five years earlier, in 2001, United Press International, in its Capital Comment column, had noted, "A source tells UPI the president ended a recent energy policy meeting with Vice President Dick Cheney and others by jokingly offering his own personal stores of 'natural gas' to help alleviate the energy crisis."

That same year, when Nancy Bagley, *Washington Life* magazine's editor in chief, interviewed former columnist Lloyd Grove for the September 2001 issue, he told her about one item the *Washington Post* wouldn't let him print: "About halfway through the general election campaign of 2000, I got word or shall I say, got wind of the fact that George W. Bush thought it was funny to punctuate a joke by breaking wind in groups of people. I first heard a story that during the campaign he called a new desk aide of Karl Rove's into his office to give him an 'Austin Welcome.'"

"Oh, you're kidding," Bagley exclaimed.

Grove wasn't. "It finally got to the point," he continued, "where [White House press secretary] Ari Fleischer was calling to deny it up and down, after some rather nondenial denials from the principal himself. And then later on, [Bush] was doing an interview on [Air Force One] with a news-magazine reporter where he ended up adjusting the air nozzle on the plane. He said he had just broken wind and that part is off the record." Grove added that during one of Dick Cheney's secret meetings with energy leaders, "Bush joked that perhaps his own natural gas was meant to be harnessed to solve the energy problem." But even though Grove had "multiple witnesses to various [similar] behaviors," his editors at the *Post* "thought it was pushing the envelope a little too far, and I can't quarrel with that."

Venezuelan president Hugo Chavez, a Bush nemesis, created a media uproar when he addressed the United Nations in New York City on September 20, 2006, the day after Bush had spoken at the same podium. "The devil came here yesterday," Chavez said. "And it smells of sulfur still today." The press took it as a figurative attack, but maybe the U.S. president had actually left a lingering air bomb for him.

In his book *State of Denial*, former *Washington Post* reporter Bob Woodward recounted how Bush pranked his chief political adviser and dirty trickster, Karl Rove, with a device called the Fart Machine. "Bush and Rove in particular dwelled on 'flatulence'—passing gas—and they shared an array of fart jokes," Woodward wrote. "The son of one senior White House staffer had a small toy with a remote control that produced a farting sound. The staffer brought it to the White House and placed it under Rove's chair for the morning senior staff meeting on July 7 [2005]." However, when Bush received news that terrorists had set off bombs in the London subways that morning and killed dozens of passengers, the big surprise was postponed for a couple of weeks. Then, "on July 20 the device was placed under Rove's chair and activated during the senior staff meeting. There were multiple activations, and it took Rove several minutes to locate the toy. Everyone laughed. They needed the humor, one of Bush's top advisers recalled."

Notorious for giving people unflattering nicknames, the president often referred to Rove as "turd blossom." It became such a popular epithet around Washington that when Slate.com writer Timothy Noah called for Rove's resignation in a 2005 article, he headlined it "Turd Blossom Must Go!" Republican insiders played down the turd blossom business, calling it an endearing Texas term for a flower that grows out of a cow patty in a pasture; but as blogger Barry Popik pointed out, "'Turd blossom' was used in 1960s Texas high school slang to describe the spreading smell of a fart, or the spreading stain of a loose bowel movement. Neither Rove nor George W. Bush attended high school in Texas, and they may have been unfamiliar with the original use of the word. 'Fart blossom' was a common variant." I, Jim Dawson, can personally corroborate Popik's statement by attesting that a turd blossom was also a fart in West Virginia high schools in the early sixties, so I'm guessing it was used elsewhere in the country.

Apparently George Bush was familiar with the Fart Machine before it was used on Rove. In 2003 his cousin, health-care executive Jonathan S. Bush, told Lloyd Grove, who was working at the time for the *New York Daily News*, that his own father, Jonathan J. Bush, stockpiled Fart Machines at his home in Connecticut and gave them away as gag gifts. "Flatulation devices—that's the clinical term," Jonathan S. said. "My father likes to make people laugh with hilarious jokes. Ever since his brother George [the First] was in the White House [1989–1992], his great claim has always been that he is one joke removed from the presidency."

It sounds like fart humor runs in the Bush DNA. According to biographer Kitty Kelley in her book *The Family: The Real Story of the Bush Dynasty*, "*The New Yorker*'s Brendan Gill, who once visited the family compound at Kennebunkport [Maine], told a . . . story about the Bushes and their disinterest in books. The writer, an insomniac, tried to find something to read late at night. After investigating the entire mansion, he could find only one book: *The Fart Book* [by Donald Wetzel]." I should add that *The Fart Book* is basically a small paperback of cartoons illustrating the many varieties, accompanied with gag lines, as in "the Bathtub Fart—the only fart you can see."

A couple of years before his presidency, when Bush was running for his second term as governor of Texas, his inaugural theme, "Together We Can," was translated for the state's many Mexican-American voters into "*Juntos Podemos.*" Unfortunately, the *Houston Chronicle* misspelled the phrase as "*Juntos Pedemos*"—which means "Together We Fart." (Luckily for Barack Obama, no one made the same mistake with his 2008 presidential theme and turned "Yes We Can" into "Yes We Fart.")

Farting, according to some experts, fits right in with George W. Bush's personality profile. Psychiatrist Justin A. Frank, who analyzed the president in his 2004 book *Bush on the Couch*, noted that "Bush's attempts at humor often harbor further traces of his contempt—both for the people he ridicules to get laughs, and for the whole notion of honest, generative discourse." In other words, his gas-passing displays were power plays, similar to the antics of an earlier president, Lyndon B. Johnson, who often dragged people into the bathroom in the midst of conversations. Johnson aide Richard Goodwin and his wife, historian Doris Kearns Goodwin, have both written at length about LBJ's penchant for talking to his staff while he took a crap. Perhaps future Bush biographers will likewise give his shit-stinking shenanigans a greater historical significance.

Who knows, George W. Bush's most memorable legacy may be the lifelike, battery-operated "Pull My Finger President" doll that farts and shakes as it utters one-liners in a mimicry of his voice, such as "That's what I call the Flatulation Proclamation!" and "Hey, Saddam, here's a weapon of mass destruction!" when you tug his outstretched index finger. In other words, as current events fade into dim historical memory, our grandchildren may think of Bush mostly as a flatulent dummy.

3

GASSY HOUND IS HOLLYWOOD BOUND!

The boys are the Jonas Brothers—Nick, Joe, and Kevin—direct from suburban New Jersey by way of the Magic Kingdom. You couldn't meet a nicer bunch of rock 'n' roll kids, as bright and squeaky clean as their toothy smiles. Raised and home-schooled by evangelical Christians, the Jonas lads celebrated at MTV's raucous Video Music Awards in 2008 by flashing purity rings, symbols of their pledge to remain virgins until marriage. *Rolling Stone* anointed them with a cover story in mid-2008 and another one in mid-2009. Though the siblings are more like clones of the Osmond kids from the 1970s, music industry flacks prefer to compare their ecstatic effect on young girls to Beatlemania and give them individual identities similar to what the 1964 teen press bestowed upon John Lennon, Paul McCartney, George Harrison, and Ringo Starr. Nick Jonas is "the serious one," Kevin "the crazy one," Joe "the cool one"; "the cute one" and "the quiet one" had already been taken by Beatles Paul and George, and nobody wanted to appropriate "the lucky one" (Ringo). By early 2009 the first three Jonas Brothers albums, released during the three previous years, had simultaneously gathered near the top of Nielsen SoundScan's Top 10, and their singles were hitting number one on the iTunes chart as regularly as Walt Disney's Hollywood Records put them out.

Meanwhile, the Mickey Mouse machine was love-bombing eleven-year-old girls with special Jonas moments on cable TV's Disney Channel and with a theatrical concert film in 3-D. But eventually, to keep up with Hollywood's Joneses, it came time for the Jonases to rise to the next level. Back in 1964 the Fab Four had starred in their own classic film comedy, *A Hard Day's Night*. So now, in 2009, the Prefab Three needed a similar cinema debut—something that would solidify their popularity among young girls, express their Christian values, and convince the general public that they were serious (yet hilariously endearing) young artists and not just flashes in the pandemic of celebuzoids. How about a movie adapted from a popular book? Okay, the romantic *Twilight* vampire series was already taken, and *The Brothers Karamazov* seemed a little too dark for the sunny trio, so what was the next best thing?

How about a tale of a dog with a severe intestinal gas problem? After all, when pubescent girls wish upon a star, they're hoping to see cute, cuddly boys and hear cute, cuddly farts, right?

Walter the Farting Dog is a best-selling children's book starring a crepitating canine who saves himself from being sent to the pound by fending off two bungling burglars with his gut gusts and sending them "choking and gasping" into the long arms of the law (for more on Walter, see "Best-Selling Dog Farts at Man" in *Blame It on the Dog*). The book's million-dollar success spawned not only several sequels but a half dozen kiddie copycats about backfiring bears, farting felines, and adorable tykes with turbulent *tuchuses*. Perhaps now, nearly a decade after *Walter* first saw print, the hapless mutt was ready for his close-up.

On October 27, 2008, *Variety* broke the big news: "Fox has locked the Jonas Brothers to make their feature-starring debut in *Walter the Farting Dog*. Based on a best-selling series of books by William Kotzwinkle and Glenn Murray, the film is being adapted by Alec Sokolow [*Toy Story*] and Joel Cohen [*Garfield*] into a family film that will revolve around Nick, Joe and Kevin Jonas, as well as their younger brother Frankie"—who was being hyped as "the bonus Jonas." Shooting was scheduled to begin in the spring of 2009.

If anyone wondered how the Jonas Brothers' wholesomeness would square with the theme of a dog that can't stop pumping clouds of really bad gas from his fart flume, they were further flummoxed by 20th Century Fox's decision to assign it to middle-aged filmmakers Peter and Bobby Farrelly, whose previous productions include the R-rated *There's Something About Mary*, infamous for Cameron Diaz's unknowingly using Ben Stiller's semen as hair gel, and the PG-13 *Dumb and Dumber*, which got its biggest laugh when Jim Carrey rolled on his back in front of a group of college kids and tried to set his farts on fire. But then again, who better to trumpet the travails and triumphs of being celebrity brothers than two other celebrity brothers who, incidentally, were in preproduction at the time for *The Three Stooges*, a film about yet another set of celebrity brothers (Moe, Shemp, and Curly Howard, née Horwitz)?

As director Peter Farrelly described the *Walter the Farting Dog* plot to *Variety*, "The brothers play musicians whose parents are asked to care for the dog by an aunt just before she passes away. By the time they've driven the dog home, everybody's head is out the window of the family station wagon but Frankie, and only because he has a serious sinus problem and doesn't notice the stench coming from Walter." Apparently eight-year-old Frankie was being consigned to Ringo Starr's fourth-banana role in *A Hard Day's Night*: "While his brothers play music, Frankie and the gaseous hound get involved in a plot that involves liberating a koi fish and thwarting jewel thieves."

The blogosphere lit up when the story broke. Derek Weiler of Canada's Quillblog (quillandquire.com) commented that for anyone who wondered what would make *Walter the Farting Dog* even better "and answered themselves, the Jonas Brothers, it's a banner day." Meanwhile, entertainment blog AnythingHollywood.com asked: "Will [the Jonases] have to go back and remake their 2006 single, 'Time for Me to Fly,' as 'Time for Me to Let One Fly'? Will their 'Hold On' be rerecorded as 'Hold On, Here Comes Another One'?"

Walter's cocreator, Glenn Murray, said he was happy that his book was being adapted into a rock musical. "It's great to have the Jonas Brothers involved in the movie," he told Canada's CBC News. "Kids know the Jonas Brothers who don't know Walter, and kids who know Walter probably all know the Jonas Brothers. So it's a win-win situation."

Despite 20th Century Fox's early estimate that *Walter* would go into production by early 2009, it remains "in development" at this writing and may not start filming until 2011. The only question left now is, what's next from the Disney dream factory? An unreliable rumor has it that Miley Cyrus, aka Hannah Montana, is gearing up to create a rumpus in the lead role of *Le Petomane's Daughter*.

4

WAR OF THE WHOOPEE WHOPPERS

In 2003 an urban legend was going around that a duck's quack doesn't echo. You'd generally find this factoid in an email message caroming around in cyberspace, loaded up with such arcane info-bits as "Butterflies taste with their feet" and "Niagara Falls is the only North American landmark that moves backward; water rushing over its rim erodes away two-and-a-half feet a year." They sound eccentric enough to be true, and probably most of them are. But Professor Trevor Cox, an acoustics engineer at the University of Salford's Acoustics Research Centre in Manchester, England, had a problem with the idea that a quack lacked slapback reverberation, and with the help of various sound chambers, a powerful computer, and a duck named Daisy, he debunked it as a mallard canard. "I [tried] to find the source of this myth because it was bugging me," he told Chris Smith of TheNakedScientists.com in 2006. "Any sound echoes, but it might be that in the case of the duck, they're very hard to hear." That's because the long "aaaacckkk" at the end of the quack tends to cover up the echo.

Given the fact that human farts and duck quacks are sometimes indistinguishable (especially in the shower), it seems only reasonable that Professor Cox would soon find himself back in the news dealing with the acoustical qualities of flatulence—or rather, the simulacra of flatulence—that is, faux farts, courtesy of the whoopee cushion.

A whoopee cushion is an airbag that makes the rude sounds of air being squeezed through a tight, squeaky exit whenever somebody sits on it. Its ancestor is the medieval pig bladder that jesters reportedly used to entertain royal courts. Commercially it hit the big time in 1930 when the JEM Rubber Company in Toronto devised a flat, hard-rubber balloon with an attached wooden mouth. After experimenting with a couple of names, JEM dubbed the little squawk bag the Whoopee Cushion. The word *whoopee* goes back to the sixteenth-century *whoup*, or *whoop*, defined as a spontaneous exclamation, usually with a vowel added, as in "whoop hooe," as Gabriel Harvey used it in 1595 to describe the sounds of boys playing in London's streets. By the late 1920s, thanks in part to the popular Broadway play *Whoopee* and Eddie Cantor's hit single "Makin' Whoopee," it was a buzz word for sex, money, and the anything-goes atmosphere that characterized the roaring decade before the bottom dropped out in 1929. The Whoopee Cushion eventually became such an everyday novelty item that its name encompassed all similar rubber noisemakers, hence the current generic lower case. But nobody ever gave the whoopee cushion much respect until Professor Cox came along.

A reasonable-looking gentleman in his early forties, Trevor Cox is an acoustics specialist and concert hall designer who, despite his whimsical bent, isn't the sort of bloke who just farts around. "The whoopee cushion has much in common with the human voice and how wind instruments work, so it is a memorable way of portraying some important science," he told Matthew Moore of London's *Daily Telegraph* in 2009.

He studied the dynamics of various whoopee cushions and designed his own "optimized" version with a bigger and better sound. Along the way he wrote several scientific papers, including "A New Paradigm for Achieving Realistic Flatulent Sounds," which appeared in the journal *Nature* in 2007. But best of all, he built the world's largest whoopee cushion: a reddish-orange rubber blob roughly the size of a bean-bag chair that an adult can comfortably lie on. "It is made out of one piece of latex and was about [six-plus feet] in diameter," Professor Cox told me in a July 2009 email. "The design was simple, because Guinness World Records expects a scaled-up replica."

His reason for building such a device, besides garnering the Guinness World Record for Biggest Whoopee Cushion, was to illustrate two back-to-back science lectures called "Beautiful Music, Horrible Sounds" that he gave to 4,500 schoolchildren, ages seven to fourteen, at London's Royal Albert Hall on October 5, 2006. As he told Chris Smith, "The mouthpieces of wind instruments such as trumpets and . . . your vocal cords, all behave using the same science as a whoopee cushion, which is the Bernoulli effect."

According to this principle, formulated by eighteenth-century Swiss mathematician Daniel Bernoulli, the speed of flowing liquid or gas is determined by density and pressure. When I later asked Professor Cox how it applied to whoopee cushions, he explained, "When the air is moving between the two sheets of rubber, it has a lower density. This means there is a lower pressure [inside] the rubber. The higher pressure outside causes the rubber sheets to slam shut." To illustrate the Bernoulli effect to the kids in such a massive venue as the Royal Albert Hall, "I needed a prop that was big and impressive." Hence "the world's largest whoopee cushion." His aim, as he advertised on the University of Salford's webpage, was "to fascinate, amuse, and inspire" kids "by exploring what sound is, why different sounds provoke positive and negative reactions, and how technology can be used to make sounds nicer—or nastier."

He carried out several acoustical demonstrations, including a test to find "the worst sound in the world," which turned out to be not the ripping of a fart but rather a toss-up between human retching (itself a toss-up, you might say) and the shrieks of a Tasmanian devil, a marsupial that's really scary even when it's quiet. But the whopping whoopee cushion is what landed him on the front pages of several British dailies.

To paraphrase John Lennon, now we know how many farts it takes to fill the Albert Hall.

The giant air bag was such a hit that Professor Cox's friend and associate, physicist Steve Mesure, built a replica and took it on the road as part of a British Council Science Alive 2007 tour, peregrinating as far as Hong Kong and inviting thousands of spectators to flop onto its welcoming folds and make a large and joyful noise.

However, the prospect of owning an even bigger "world's biggest" rubber razzer became too irresistible for Mesure, so he built a new one that was nearly ten feet in diameter. During the BBC Philharmonic's Comic Relief charity performance of Tchaikovsky's *1812 Overture* in March 2009, Mesure's new Guinness World Record holder stood in for the traditional artillery piece during the finale, as five young beauties from a girl band called the Saturdays took turns throwing themselves onto it to create a cannonade of raspberries. But Professor Cox remained sanguine. "My two-meter [cushion] is actually a better stage prop," he said. "[Mesure's] three-meter one is too big."

But wait! The world had not yet heard the last of Trevor Cox. Ever the inquiring scientist, he set out to discover the world's funniest-sounding fart. But that's a later chapter.

5

MY CHAIR IS TELLING EVERYONE I STINK!

In March 2009, CareerBuilder.com ran an article on AOL called "6 Examples of Workplace Rudeness," spotlighting office behaviors that everyone should avoid. For example, don't interrupt when other people are talking; don't leave the lunchroom messier than you found it; don't talk loudly on the phone; and never use profanity, unless you happen to be working for Larry Flynt. But nowhere on that list was, "Don't fart in your chair and brag about it."

Granted, most office workers try to hide their flatulence. In fact, a small, specialized industry sprang up more than a dozen years ago to provide activated-charcoal and foam seat cushions that muffle the sound (like gun-barrel silencers) and soak up the scent of ass gas (like cigarette filters).

But Randy Sarafan, a San Francisco–based technological gadfly and self-proclaimed "interstellar wrecking ball," believes that he should not only fart proudly at the office but also send every butt burst beaming out into the world. That's why he hot-rodded and hot-wired his seat to create what he calls the Twittering Office Chair, which detects his natural gas, posts each poot at http://twitter.com/officechair, and sends them out to, at last count, more than three thousand "followers" throughout the Twitterverse.

For the non-Internet-savvy, Twitter is a social networking service that lets people send and read each others' "tweets"—instant messages restricted to 140 characters, delivered to all who have agreed to receive them. Since its creation in 2006, Twitter has gone worldwide and, as of early 2009, gets fifty-five million visits every month. If Twitter is basically an "addiction to constant self-affirmation," as the cartoon site SuperNews! (current.com/supernews) puts it, then nothing is more self-affirming than the idea that everybody is dying to hear about your farts the moment they happen.

Randy Sarafan outfitted his chair with a gas sensor and an electronic communications system because, as he says on his webpage, "I am a gassy individual. Since my flatulence is a part of life, it would be fraudulent of me to document life as it happens without documenting these occurrences."

When he blissfully lets one go in his chair, his gas activates one of ten random bittersweet Twitter tweets from his chair's point of view. The original ones included:

• *Pfffffffft.*

• *Someone please disassemble me.*

• *I wish I were some other chair.*

• *He farted right on me again.*

• *Allow me to repeat . . . ppppfffffffffftttttttttttt.*

Since then Randy has added a few more, including, "Is it the weekend yet?" Here's a suggestion for one more that I willingly donate to his cause: "Whoops, he just shit himself."

You can follow Randy's guide and make your own auto-tooting device, should you have an office chair, a natural gas sensor, a SquidBee (a wireless transmitter), a computer with the Python program, a sharp tool to create a pocket within the seat cushion, and a few other necessary items—not to mention a powerful desire to share your gastrointestinal disturbances with friends and strangers alike. Simply go to Instructables.com/id/The-Twittering-Office-Chair.

Randy's page has generated plenty of comments. Twitter user Mephedaw sarcastically congratulated him with "Over 3000 people are following your farts wow." MegaMaker wrote, "Congrats, you can now send 'twoots.'" Frenchelbow wondered, "But does it go far enough? Why not something that twitters internally? You could add a sensor to the pink folds of your colon." But Thepelton probably came up with the most cogent observation: "This is one of those times that you actually can feel good that someone hasn't figured out how to transmit smell over the net."

Love him or loathe him, you must admit that Randy Sarafan's tweetings are no more banal than the overwhelming majority of the nattering, chattering, and time-frittering patter being Twittered, Flickred, Facebooked, and blogged every moment of the day and night. Though Twitter proved itself politically invaluable to tens of thousands of Iranian street protesters in the summer of 2009, it's mostly, as multiplatinum singer John Mayer complained to E! Online, "one step away from posting pictures of your poop."

6

HIS TOOTING DID THE TALKING

Call it the "Pig Pen effect," after the *Peanuts* comic strip character who carried a swirling dust cloud around with him. If you want to keep people at arm's length, or even farther away, simply encase yourself in an aura of filth. Look grungy and stink.

A renowned child psychologist named Dr. Mara Sidoli found her own Pig Pen in the early 1990s. He was a hyperactive seven-year-old boy named Peter. He was born prematurely, and when he was only a few months old, Social Services permanently took him away from his neglectful mother. Over the next few years, when he wasn't in the hospital recovering from one of his many surgeries, he lived with an adoptive family that didn't quite know what to do with him. Life had dealt Peter a lousy hand, and he was pretty unhappy about it. Bereft of any intimate human bond, he withdrew deeper into himself and reacted aggressively, sometimes violently, to those who tried to reach him. Finally his adoptive parents took him to Dr. Sidoli, a psychology professor at the University of New Mexico in Albuquerque who maintained a private practice in Santa Fe, sixty miles away.

Dr. Sidoli was born in Italy in 1937 and trained in England as a Jungian therapist. Carl Jung, the Swiss acolyte and later rival of Sigmund Freud upon whose work Jungian therapy is based, postulated that the way to find deeper meaning and a healthy relationship with others was to tap into one's own "collective unconscious": an underworld of common symbols from dreams, myths, and folklore. This "archetypal imagery," as Jung called it, was viewed as something that all humans share from earliest childhood.

Peter was a difficult patient who "lived in a world dominated by bizarre archetypical fantasies and persecutory hallucinations," Dr. Sidoli would later write in a British journal. "Peter held loud conversations with imaginary beings and made loud anal farts as well as farting noises with his mouth whenever he became anxious or angry." He claimed that his farts were "lethal gas with which he was poisoning me. Then he would warn me that the gas was on the way, and that I should wear a gas mask."

Dr. Sidoli determined that Peter was creating a "defensive olfactive container using his bodily smell and farts to envelop himself in a protective cloud of familiarity against the dread of falling apart, and to hold his personality together." In other words, the boy wasn't able to articulate his insecurity and sense of endangerment, so he just let his body odors scare people away. "Like a skunk, he both protected himself and attacked his enemies with a barrier of poisonous smell," she said.

Under normal circumstances, luxuriating in one's own atmosphere of flatulence is a guilty pleasure, kind of like sniffing your armpits or smelling your finger after you've rubbed it between your toes or inside your belly button. Come on, admit it, your farts have a rich and heady bouquet, whereas everybody else's have a really nasty stench. But Peter, wrapped in a noxious cocoon, was being a little extreme. Naturally it all went back to his infancy, when he was separated from his mother. The olfactory sense is very well developed in babies, Dr. Sidoli observed, and with Peter "the loss of the mother's familiar smell was substituted, in an autistic way, by the smells from his own body."

Her breakthrough came one day when Peter was being especially obnoxious. Remembering a classic case in which Dr. Jung calmed a violent female patient by threatening to hit her back if she struck him, "I decided to counteract," Dr. Sidoli wrote. "I altered my technique and acted out his

own games for him, including the making of loud fart noises of my own."
Peter became angrier, ordered her to stop, and physically attacked her, but
she continued to mock him with her own flatulent noises, just to show him
how ridiculous they were. "After a while he gave me a long, steady look," she
said, "and then burst out in wholehearted laughter."

After that session, his behavior began to improve. Peter later bonded
with his adoptive parents and eventually left therapy.

The stink really hit the fan after Dr. Sidoli wrote about Peter's "defen-
sive autistic barrier of farts" in an article called "Farting as a Defence
Against Unspeakable Dread" in the April 1996 issue of the London-based
Journal of Analytical Psychology (that's Volume 41, Number 2, if you're going
through your pile of magazines; it's on page 165). The folks at Harvard
University's humor and science magazine, *Annals of Improbable Research*
(AIR), got wind of the case study a year later and nominated Dr. Sidoli for
an Ig Nobel Prize, AIR's spoof of the Nobel Prize that honors imaginative
and goofy achievements in science, medicine, and technology. When the
awards—trophies of a nearly naked man—were handed out on October
8, 1998, at Harvard's Sanders Theatre, Dr. Sidoli's "Farting as a Defence
Against Unspeakable Dread" didn't win the Prize for Medicine (that honor
went to an article in the *Lancet* medical journal called "A Man Who Pricked
His Finger and Smelled Putrid for 5 Years"), but rather for Literature, as
if Peter were the antagonist of some Jungian fable. One can only wonder
whether Dr. Jung himself, who died in 1961 and never met Dr. Mara Sidoli,
would have approved.

Most of her casework with Peter ended up in her book *When the Body
Speaks: The Archetypes in the Body*, published in 2000, just before she died
from a lingering illness. Peter's current whereabouts are unknown. Who
knows, maybe Peter was just his case-study name. Maybe he's really that
guy who built the Twitter office chair.

7

THE (BUTT) CRACK OF DAWN

In Great Britain and parts of the Commonwealth—namely New Zealand and Australia—a fairly popular slang expression is "sparrow fart," as when a cobber, a bloke, or a mate might say, "We'll be up at sparrow fart." It's the earliest time of the morning, when all the awakening sparrows chirp from their bottoms to greet a glorious new day. Or so it's claimed. We don't really know if sparrows fart at all (they have an all-purpose cloaca, not an anus per se), much less fart first thing before sunrise, but because one of the first things we humans do when we stir is to blast away the night's accumulation of internal gases, we expect the same from our feathered friends.

If the little critters are already filling the air with birdsong when you wake up, you've missed sparrow fart.

Sparrow fart—sometimes hyphenated, sometimes possessive (sparrow's fart)—is generally used in a jocular way, as in, "You mean I have to be up at sparrow fart?" It most likely came from an observation that the early morning was so quiet you could hear a birdy break wind. Why a sparrow and not an owl? Well, sparrows, which exist all over the world in many varieties, are generally small birds whose farts must be ethereal and subsonic. The air would have to be deathly still for even the most sensitive ears to pick up such a teensy-weensy butt whisper. We Americans would say, "It's so quiet you could hear a pin drop." Thus sparrow fart is that very moment that separates the tranquility of night from the clatter of dawn, or as the American novelist Thomas Wolfe chanted a couple of times in *Look Homeward, Angel*, "In that enormous silence, birds were waking."

The *Oxford English Dictionary* doesn't mention any sparrows' farts, though it does cite an obsolete sixteenth-century term, "sparrow-blasted," which means to be blighted by an insignificant or nonexistent power, as in, "No more praying against thunder and lightning, than by sparrow-blasting," from 1589. (In other words, a prayer or a sparrow's fart will get you the same result; it's the Elizabethan equivalent of "worth about as much as a fart in a windstorm.") But "sparrow fart" has been in colloquial use since at least the early nineteenth century, according to William Carr's *Craven Dialect* (1824), which pinpoints it as a Yorkshire creation meaning "break of day." British troops popularized it during WWI, but veterans had to yield to the more printable "sparrow crack" in their postwar memoirs, as when Major Ardern Hume Beaman, in *The Squadroon* (1920), wrote, "Well, we've got to get up at sparrow crack—train goes at half-five." *Crack*, or *cracke*, is a synonym for the verb *fart* going back to the seventeenth century; Thomas Urquhart, in his 1653 English translation of Rabelais's *Gargantua and Pantagruel*, used the word to replace the Latin phrase *crepitum reddere* (to break wind) in the line: "Then he . . . belched, cracked, yawned."

In fact, the American term for sparrow fart is "the crack of dawn," which originally referred not to an early-morning backfire but rather to the small wedge of light that first appears on the eastern horizon as the sun begins to rise. It may come from the archaic English expression "the crack of doom"; that is, the biblical "thunder-peal of the day of judgment," as the *Oxford English Dictionary* puts it. But in recent times we have made the various "cracks" cruder and ruder. A more modern British variant is a redundant "the crack of sparrow fart," whereas Americans now call it the "butt-crack (or ass-crack) of dawn," referring not to a fart but rather to the cleft from which it comes.

The sparrow fart may not be heard, but you can find it all around. Scottish mystery writer Stuart MacBride wrote on his blog in 2009, "The next morning I was up at sparrow's fart to catch an obscenely early train to Edinburgh." In 1993 Australian novelist Patti Walkuski moaned in *No Bed of Roses: Memoirs of a Madam*: "I was sick of working from sparrow fart as station cook and general dogs-body." And on BBC TV's 1980s cult program, *Minder*, actor George Cole's Arthur Daly character routinely uttered such lines as, "You'd have to be up at sparrow's fart to get in on that."

The Irish, however, have a different meaning. For them a sparrow fart is not early morning but an annoying or inconsequential person. Dublin novelist James Joyce put it into the mind of Molly Bloom during her stream-of-consciousness soliloquy near the end of *Ulysses*: "Miss This Miss That Miss Theother lot of sparrowfarts skitting around talkin about politics they know as much about as my backside."

You'll have to get up pretty early in the morning to find anyone who celebrates the expression more than New Zealanders. They've put it on a postage stamp. (See it for yourself at electricearl.com/fart/duck.html.) "If you wake up at sparrow fart, are away with the fairies, get stuck in boots and all, or are prone to throwing a hissy fit, you are, like the latest issue of New Zealand Post stamps, a classic Kiwi," wrote the New Zealand Post in 2007. "The new stamps have an added twist—people can rub off the black mark to reveal the definition of the expressions." (The translations are "so early even the birds are asleep," "traveling far away," "throwing yourself enthusiastically into an activity," and "losing your temper.")

When I contacted Post Stamp General Manager Ivor Masters two years later to see how the sparrow's fart stamp was doing, he responded that the issue had sold very well to both collectors and regular stamp users, but since all of the stamps were sold as a full sheet, "it is impossible for us to identify sales of the 'sparrow fart' themselves." Oddly enough, although Masters and the Post press releases consistently called the dark, beautiful stamp a "sparrow fart," it actually says "sparrow's fart." But New Zealanders didn't complain one way or the other. "We did receive a couple of letters with reference to sparrow fart but no more letters than other stamp issues," said Masters. "The term sparrow fart is quite common in New Zealand and I would say it's generally accepted as part of our language." In other words, he didn't hear a peep from anyone.

If the U.S. Postal Service ever similarly issued a set with American colloquialisms, you can bet that the "Fart in a Windstorm" first-class stamp would keep talk-radio goobers and their brethren in the pulpits foaming at the mouth for weeks. Which goes to show you just how much more evolved those Kiwis be. After all, if God's eye is on the sparrow, His ear must be on the sparrow's fart—and so far *He* hasn't fussed about it.

8

BUTT BLASTS BRING DOWN AMERICAN AIRLINER!

You should probably light a match after you've dropped a really stinky fart (or a stinky turd) within a confined area—unless you're on an airplane.

It was a clear, early Monday morning, December 4, 2006. American Airlines Flight 1053 from Washington, D.C., to Dallas/Fort Worth was already at maximum altitude when several passengers complained to a flight attendant that they could smell burning sulfur.

The crew went into emergency mode. Only four months earlier, British police had foiled a terrorist plot to blow up at least seven passenger aircraft over the Atlantic with homemade chemicals smuggled aboard in soft-drink and shampoo bottles. U.S. and British authorities had immediately banned all liquids, including water, hair gels, and lotions, from carry-on luggage. Also fresh in the minds of American Airlines employees was British jihadist wannabe Richard Reid, who had tried to light his explosive tennis shoes with matches on an American Airlines flight from Paris to Miami on Christmas Day 2001. Fortunately, an alert flight attendant who smelled what she thought was a burnt match coming from Reid's row had sicced a couple of male passengers on him before he could blow himself up.

Given this heightened sense of danger, the Flight 1053 pilot notified Federal Aviation Administration authorities at 6:30 a.m. about the mysterious sulfuric fumes in the passenger section. They ordered an emergency landing in Nashville. FBI agents evacuated all ninety-nine passengers into the terminal, while bomb-sniffing dogs were rushed aboard the plane.

As Nashville International Airport Authority spokeswoman Lynne Lowrance would later tell *The Tennessean* reporter Samuel Shu, agents found "evidence of where matches had been struck in an individual's seating area." During interrogation, the passenger, a Dallas woman, confessed that she had lighted several matches to cover up a couple of really bad farts, essentially replacing one sulfuric residue with another. It was an attempt to conceal a "body odor" caused by a "medical condition," Ms. Lowrance said. Though the lady's turbulence problem was unspecified, it was most likely an irritable bowel disorder, such as Crohn's disease, that makes it difficult to maintain a holding pattern during a flight. But still, said Lowrance, "It's unusual that someone would go to those measures to cover it up."

When authorities finally cleared Flight 1053 for takeoff, they didn't allow the woman back on the plane. She wasn't charged but could have been, because although it's legal to bring as many as four books of paper safety matches onto an aircraft, it is illegal to strike even one of them.

When Shu's story went out on the wire, the national media had a field day. Mainstream outlets such as ABC News and the *Washington Post* played it straight, but *Chicago Sun-Times* columnist Mark Brown dubbed the report "Farts on a plane"—after the title of the recent action film *Snakes on a Plane*—and subheaded it: "One man's laughing gas becomes one woman's stink bomb!" According to Brown, "Some may find it surprising that the culprit here was a woman. Not me. A man most likely would have either tried to pretend all along that he didn't do it—or that it didn't stink. From among the options a man might consider, lighting a match would have finished far below bragging about it."

Ultra-conservative blogger Debbie Schlussel felt that the American crew had overreacted. "Who would make you feel less safe on a flight?" she demanded on her website. "[A] farting lady with body odor due to a medical condition beyond her control; or . . . six extremist Muslim imams who imitate the 9/11 hijackers, ask for seatbelt extenders that could be used to strangle passengers, take unauthorized seating patterns suitable for hijacking, verbally attack America, and have ties to Hamas, Al-Qaeda, and other groups whose *raison d'etre* is 'Death to America'?"

Schlussel was referring to an event two weeks earlier, on November 20, in which a passenger aboard a US Airways flight at Minneapolis–St. Paul International had written a hasty message to the pilot before take-off about "6 suspicious Arab men on plane, spaced out in their seats." A couple of them had asked for eighteen-inch seat-belt extenders, and an Arabic-speaking passenger had heard one of them cursing Americans. The note writer thought they might be on a dry run for a future hijack mission. Security police came aboard and took the Muslims off the plane, and the FBI detained them for several hours. Their attorney later told CNBC that the six were planning to hit the airline with a huge lawsuit.

Schlussel was outraged that these six "flying imams" were going to come out smelling like a rose, while the poor Texas tooter was grounded. "Who's more dangerous?" she asked. "We know the answer."

Incidentally, this wasn't the first time such boorish behavior had disrupted a flight. Back in April 1995, Reuters News Agency reported that a South African Airways jetliner on its way from London to Johannesburg with three hundred human passengers was forced to turn back and make an emergency landing after "the collective [body] heat and methane" of seventy-two prize stud pigs in the cargo hold triggered the plane's automatic fire control system, which included the release of oxygen-replacing halon gas. The halon, not the methane, asphyxiated fifteen of the pigs. Why were these pigs—even prized ones—flying on a commercial airline? According to a company spokesman, traveling on a passenger flight was more direct and thus "less traumatic for the pigs than going on a freighter flight."

The moral is clear: farts on a plane can really bring you down.

9

THE WORLD'S OLDEST FART JOKE

Who knew that "Here I sit all broken-hearted, tried to shit but only farted" has a long and reputable pedigree?

Britain's Reuters News Agency announced on July 31, 2008, that researchers had found the world's oldest recorded joke in southern Iraq, in what was once Sumeria—and it was a fart joke! The roughly four-thousand-year-old fart joke had probably been written between 1900 and 2004 B.C.E.

The University of Wolverhampton in England enshrined it at the pinnacle of its Top 10 list of really hoary jokes, way ahead of the 1600 B.C.E. Egyptian quip about King Snofru that went: "How do you entertain a bored pharaoh? You sail a boatload of young women dressed only in fishing nets down the Nile and urge the pharaoh to go catch a fish." And it was millennia ahead of the oldest known British joke, from the tenth century, that asked, "What hangs at a man's thigh and wants to poke the hole that it has often poked before?" "A key."

Now, are you ready for the world's most ancient fart joke?

It was a Sumerian proverb written on wet clay in cuneiform script during the Old Babylonian period, and it goes like this: "Something which has never occurred since time immemorial; a young woman did not fart in her husband's lap."

Ba-da-boom!

Well, maybe that translation is too literal. Let's try it again: "Something which has never occurred since time immemorial: a young woman who did not fart in her husband's embrace."

Hey, I'm dying up here. Is this an audience or an oil painting? How many Sumerians does it take to screw up a joke? Take my farting wife, please. Sorry, I didn't mean to babble on. Maybe you had to be there.

The Top 10's compiler, Professor Paul McDonald, told Reuters' John Joseph that jokes have always taken various forms, whether a riddle, a proverb, or a set-up question with a surprise answer. "What they all share, however, is a willingness to deal with taboos and a degree of rebellion," he said. "Modern puns, Essex girl jokes, and toilet humor can all be traced back to the very earliest jokes identified in this research."

What got Dr. McDonald started on his quest was a commission from the British comedy TV network Dave to put together a Dave Historical Humour Study and track down the world's most timeworn witticisms and bygone gags in time for the channel's August 2, 2008, celebration of stand-up comedy at New York's Apollo Theater. He and his team of academics first defined a joke as having a clear setup-and-punch-line structure. Then they spent two months trawling the annals of history, from clay tablets to Egypt's Westcar Papyrus (the source of the fishing pharaoh joke). "For the oldest they wanted something that could withstand academic scrutiny," Dr. McDonald told me in a March 2009 email, "while the rest of the top ten consists of ancient jokes that are interesting for one reason or another (e.g., because they have been offered as the oldest by other people, or because they are the first instance of a particular joke structure, etc)."

What makes this girly-poot proverb a joke, he said, is "its comic incongruity . . . its juxtaposition of the ideal and the real [which] has the latter qualifying the former in an unequivocally humorous way." He admitted that he didn't have to put on his Indiana Jones hat, smuggle himself into dusty Iraq, and find his quarry on an engraved stone guarded by a nest of vipers. He's a boffin (that's British for a scientific expert), not a buccaneer, so he simply perused many selected tomes that reprinted ancient literature, including Bendt Alster's *Proverbs of Ancient Sumer*, and there it was.

What the joke is saying is that at some point in every marriage a man will discover, to his shock and dismay, that his beautiful and pristine young bride farts just like he does—and her gas smells just as rotten as his, if not worse. Jonathan Swift picked up this trope for several parodies of romantic poetry—described in detail in *Who Cut the Cheese?*—whose sentiments include a suggestion from *Strephon and Chloe* (1734) that a young man should watch his girlfriend defecate before he marries her, just to make sure he really loves *her* instead of some idealized version of her.

The comedy writers behind HBO's *Sex and the City* laid out the same problem from a woman's point of view in a first-season episode called "The Drought." Carrie (Sarah Jessica Parker) thinks her boyfriend has lost interest in her because she accidentally let out a stinky in front of him. "This is a watershed relationship moment and I'm never going to be able to erase it," she confesses to her friend Samantha (Kim Cattrell) during a yoga class. "I farted. . . . It wasn't a choice. I'm human. It happened."

Samantha: "No, honey, you're a woman, and men don't like women to be human. We aren't supposed to fart, douche, use tampons, or have hair in places we shouldn't."

Later Carrie tells another friend, Miranda (Cynthia Nixon), "I farted. I farted in front of my boyfriend."

Miranda: "And?"

Carrie: "And we're no longer having sex, and he thinks of me as one of the boys, and I'm gonna have to move to another city where the shame of this won't follow me."

Miranda: "You farted. You're human."

Carrie: "I don't want him to know that."

Just between you and me, I'm aware of a joke, reportedly from one of the early Egyptian dynasties, that may even precede Dr. McDonald's Sumerian joke. It goes like this: "Yo' mummy so old she farts dust."

10

GIVING IT UP FOR LENTILS

Powerful signs and flaming visions have traditionally inspired religious and philosophical conversions. Paul of Tarsus was blinded by a heavenly luminescence on his way to Damascus. Roman Emperor Constantine saw a great burning cross in the sky. And the Greek philosopher Metrocles was called to the true meaning of his life by . . . a fart!

And nobody even had to light it first.

Granted, Metrocles' conversion wasn't religious. He became not a Christian but a Cynic, which in his day (the B.C.E. 300s) was like being a free-spirited hippie rather than today's embittered pessimist. The Cynics believed that life's purpose was to live humbly and virtuously in alignment with nature, without possessions or ambitions of pursuing wealth, power, and fame—not all that different, really, from what Jesus Christ would teach more than three centuries later. Probably the most famous Cynic was Diogenes of Sinope, a banker's son turned street bum who ambled around Athens holding a lamp, claiming to be searching for an honest man, and died around 325 B.C.E., either just before or after Metrocles was born. The word *cynic*—from the Greek *kynikos* (doggish or doglike)—may have been pinned on the Cynics by their critics, but Diogenes embraced it because he felt that man's best friend was more virtuous than man himself.

We don't know too much about Metrocles. He grew up in modest circumstances in Maroneia and moved to Athens to study at Aristotle's Lyceum. He had a hippie sister named Hipparchia who married another Cynic philosopher named Crates. Not much of Metrocles' writings have survived except for a few anecdotes.

According to Diogenes Laërtius (who lived at least five hundred years later and shouldn't be confused with his light-bearing namesake), Metrocles was a neurotic young man who became so embarrassed when he farted during a speech rehearsal at school that he shut himself in his room and vowed to starve to death as penance. Fortunately, his brother-in-law Crates stopped by to offer some good Cynical advice. Born into wealth, Crates had given it all away to live on the streets without a care. He treated everyone as an equal, regardless of social status, and dispensed acts of kindness without any thought of repayment. He explained to Metrocles that because breaking wind was part of man's nature, like breathing, how could it be a mark of shame? When these words failed to move the fasting young fart-sick fellow, Crates switched stratagems. He said something like, "Hey, I'm not gonna let you starve to death. Here, let me cook us up some lupines [lentils]." He prepared a simple repast and persuaded Metrocles to join him. An hour or two later, after more philosophical discussion, Crates lifted a cheek and blasted off a volley of lentil farts to demonstrate just how wonderful it feels to unburden oneself with great pride and gusto. Perhaps he said something on the line of, "Wow, that one sure felt good, but not half as good as this next one coming up!" or "If Diogenes were here right now, his lamp would be burning bright blue!" In any event, Crates finally convinced his brother-in-law that letting them rip was nothing to be embarrassed about. More important, his bold-faced display of flatulence brought about a valuable convert to Cynicism.

Whether this story is completely true or not, it was a useful parable for the Cynic cause. First of all, it demonstrated that despite the best classical education that Greek society could provide, Metrocles was still crippled by bourgeois, self-hating propriety. It was also a good plug for lentils—a cheap, humble, and nutritious food favored by the poor and destitute—as an antidote to the overabundance of delicacies and wines that wealthy Athenians heaped on their tables. And finally, it had just the right dose of earthy humor to make the antimaterialist lesson go down easier.

Another chronicler, the philosopher Teles, who lived a hundred years after Metrocles, painted the shamefaced Cynic in less flattering terms, as a frustrated social climber who couldn't keep up with the Lyceum's extravagant lifestyle—sort of like a ghetto or hillbilly kid today who gets a scholarship to Harvard and becomes bitter because he can't fit in. To Teles, Metrocles' conversion had more to do with sour grapes (Aesop) than lentil-fueled moral clarity (Diogenes).

Metrocles went on to live a long life and die an old fart. Biographers think he may have deliberately suffocated himself. We'll never know, but maybe he simply overindulged in lentils and fell asleep in a tiny, simple, and airtight room.

11

FARTS, PRESS 1; FOR MORE FARTS, PRESS 2

One suggestion I've gotten from dozens of readers over the years is "Why don't you put one of those little computer chips in your book so that when you open it, it farts at you?" That's not an unreasonable idea. Pooting gift cards and talking children's books have been around for years. And given the fact that many people buy fart books more for their shock value than for any elucidation, why not include an added gimmick that actually creates fart noises? For a regular trade paperback book, however, my publisher has found the cost and inconvenience of inserting a chip to be prohibitive—and it would have created a distracting lump (kind of like what a fart does sometimes). Readers would be absently fingering it the way a guy with a beard can't stop stroking his face. Besides, would you really want this book to be crepitating every time you opened it?

On the other hand, in late 2008, Chronicle Books solved the problem by marrying an electronic whoopee cushion with the printed word in a hardback book called *Farts: A Spotter's Guide*. It has been cheese-cutting into my royalties ever since—and I'm not very happy about that. Despite its dearth of pages (there are only twenty-four), this is a rather hefty tome because those pages are thick cardboard, and all of them are partly cut away so that an attached battery-powered fart machine can poke through on the right side, with a repertoire of ten numbered farts, ranging from the Aftershock (*Outburstus abrupstinkus*) to the Seismic Blast (*Stinkitupsii blowdoorsoffis*). It's the perfect gift for that person who's always saying, "I want a book that speaks to me."

Farts: A Spotter's Guide purports to be a hunter's handbook of "the natural history cannon" of flatulence. (*Spotter* has a double meaning here, of course, as anyone letting most of these farts would probably leave a few brown afterburner stains in his underwear.) "No doubt with all those grapes, Aristotle, the first naturalist, passed gas," writes Crai S. Bower, a Seattle freelancer. "And Linnaeus must have eaten too much *Solanum melongena* (aka eggplant) while working through some late-night taxonomical riddle, only to spend the following morning tooting in Latin."

The overripe text describes the range, voice, and field marks of each emanation, and Fudge Factory Comics artist Travis Millard's imaginative illustrations (black and white except for the blue fart clouds) show the offenders in their natural habitats. For example, Fart Number 5, the Flight of the Buttock Bees (*Analretentivenus producii*), better known as an office fart, ranges "from icy situations to purse-lipped environments," with a voice that has a "shrill staccato sound, suggesting air-horn pressure." To hear it for yourself, press button number 5 on the blue plastic fart machine—and yes, it is staccato.

Incidentally, by making the farts blue, Millard may have spearheaded a new trend in the graphic presentation of flatulence. In the past, farts have been rendered as green, especially in cartoons (*Ren & Stimpy*) and cartoonish films and videos (*Spawn*, Howard Stern's *Butt Bongo Fiesta*, etc.), to suggest the smell of moss or swamp water. Even Whoopi Goldberg, discussing her butt cracks in front of an audience at Montreal's Just for Laughs Gala on June 25, 2009, said, "Ever since I became menopausal, my fart gas has become a green cloud."

Farts "was inspired by my belief that the life history of passed gas was a missing study in evolution," Bower, a travel writer by trade, emailed me in late July 2009 from some exotic location where he was lavishly spending the royalties he'd diverted from my bank account. "Surely Darwin, having spent four years with Captain FitzRoy eating South American food on the HMS *Beagle*, was keenly aware of the many varieties of farts that existed. I've never understood why he spent so much time chasing finches in the Galapagos when plenty of specimens for research existed in his own cabin."

Bower says that thanks to a large order from Urban Outfitters—the clothing and home furnishings chain store known for selling controversial items like the Ghettopoly board game and Palestinian mock-terrorist T-shirts—*Farts* sold out its initial print run in a couple of weeks. Subsequent printings continue to do well, especially on Amazon, where it has been offered as part of a two-fer and three-fer with my own *Who Cut the Cheese?* The American Librarians Association selected *Farts* as a "2009 Quick Pick for Reluctant Young Adult Readers," that is, one of several dozen "books that teens, ages 12 through 18, will pick up on their own and read for pleasure," according to the ALA website. "Farting," says Bower, "is a universal language that everybody understands."

He claims that reviews have been uniformly favorable, but the most personal and satisfying came after he interviewed Dr. Daniel Rubin, a leading naturopathic oncologist in Arizona, for an article unrelated to the book. "He googled me at the end of our session and declared, 'Holy shit! You wrote the farts book? My daughter and I were looking at it just last night in Urban Outfitters. We couldn't stop laughing.' It was a very strange way to end an interview with a medical pioneer. I still owe him a signed copy."

Farts: A Spotter's Guide continues to sell in stores and on the Internet, but somehow I think it won't be available anytime soon on Kindle, unless Chronicle Books can bundle it with iFart.

12

HOUSTON, WE HAVE A PROBLEM

In Disney's 1997 film comedy *RocketMan,* Harland Williams was an astronaut walking with his commander on the surface of Mars when suddenly, thanks to "intense intestinal cramps," he blasted a turbo-charged fart in his space suit and watched a large bubble move through the oxygen tube that bound the two together. "Wasn't me!" he declared innocently, even though there wasn't another earthling within thirty-five million miles.

When President John F. Kennedy launched America's manned space program in May 1961 by promising to put a man on the moon and bring him safely back to Earth before the end of the decade, the media never broached the question that must have entered the mind of every imaginative twelve-year-old kid: If an astronaut farts in an airtight space capsule somewhere high above the Earth, how does he get rid of it? What effect would it have on the capsule's delicate atmosphere? And what about the supposed greater flammability of gases, like hydrogen and methane, in zero gravity?

According to David Michael Harland, author of *The First Men on the Moon,* NASA astronauts on at least two Apollo missions did in fact have a serious farting problem, thanks to filters that created hydrogen bubbles in their drinking water. It especially afflicted the Apollo 11 crew—Buzz Aldrin, Neil Armstrong, and Michael Collins—on their historic trip to the moon in July 1969.

During a telecast from the Columbia spacecraft on Flight Day 2 of the mission, Collins demonstrated for viewers back on Earth how they prepared their dehydrated food packets for dinner. "All you have to do is add three ounces of hot water and wait for five or ten minutes," said Collins, holding up a tube of dried chicken stew. "Now we get our hot water out of a little spigot up here with a filter on it that filters out any gases that may be in the drinking water, and we just stick the end of this little tube in the end of the spigot and pull the trigger three times for three ounces of hot water and then mush it up"—he kneaded the tube with his thumbs and forefingers to squash the lumps—"and slice the end off it, and there you go, beautiful chicken stew."

The next day, however, Collins wasn't so chipper about his freeze-dried vittles. When Bruce McCandless at Mission Control in Houston asked him, "Are you having any difficulties with gas in the food bags, like the Apollo 10 crew reported?" Collins answered, "That's intermittently affirmative, Bruce. We have these two hydrogen gas filters that work fine as long as you don't actually hook them up to a food bag. But the entry way into the food bag gives enough back pressure to cause the filters to lose efficiency."

As Collins himself would later write in his 1974 memoir *Carrying the Fire*, "The drinking water is laced with hydrogen bubbles (a consequence of fuel-cell technology which demonstrates that H_2 and O join imperfectly to form H_2O). Those bubbles produce gross flatulence in the lower bowel, resulting in a not-so-subtle and pervasive aroma reminiscent of a mixture of wet dog and marsh gas."

According to Harland, "Aldrin would later jest that by the time they were on their way home they were suffering so badly that if the [rocket control system] thrusters were to have failed, [the three astronauts] would have been able to provide manual attitude control." Though he was joking, he raised a potential danger with space flatulence: since Newton's third law of motion says, "For every action there is an equal and opposite reaction," could a fart in zero gravity inadvertently propel an astronaut forward at a critical moment when he needs to be stationary?

Despite these hydrogen-fueled discomforts, Aldrin and Armstrong took the spacecraft's lunar landing module, the LM *Eagle*, down to the surface of the moon and became the first humans to walk among the craters. It was the greatest technological achievement of the twentieth century.

In "Clinical Aspects of Crew Health," the first chapter of a 1975 paper titled *Biomedical Results of Apollo*, medical doctors W. Royce Hawkins and John F. Zieglschmid of the Lyndon B. Johnson Space Center wrote that the farting problem first showed up on Apollo 10. "This crew complained of abdominal rumblings caused by the ingestion of hydrogen gas present in the potable water. Since they were concerned that diarrhea might develop, they decided on their own initiative to take Lomotil tablets. Medically, the use of the drug was not indicated. Lomotil decreases the activity of the lower intestinal tract and reduces the amount of gas that can be expelled."

On the follow-up flight, "The Apollo 11 Commander and Lunar Module Pilot each took one Lomotil tablet to retard bowel movements before Lunar Module operations. They each carried extra Lomotil tablets into the Lunar Module but did not use them."

Neil Armstrong may have been the first man to set foot on the moon, but Buzz Aldrin was the first to pee there. He says he used the relief tube built into his spacesuit moments after stepping down onto the surface, on live TV in front of six hundred million unsuspecting earthlings. Unfortunately, there's no record of who let the first lunar fart, and frankly I'm surprised that Aldrin, who seems to have been the mission's jokester, didn't lay claim to it.

When Aldrin and Armstrong climbed back inside the *Eagle* and took off their helmets, they noticed a strong odor, which Armstrong described as "wet ashes in a fireplace" and Aldrin, in his memoirs, as "a pungent metallic smell, something like gunpowder or the smell in the air after a firecracker had gone off." No, it wasn't a hydrogen-heavy butt bog. It turned out to be the smell of moon dust. But by the time the Apollo 11 capsule returned to Earth and splashed into the Pacific, it stunk like a toilet. When a Navy frogman opened the hatch, the stench nearly knocked him into the water. What he described later was not the scent of moon dust.

None of this, of course, showed up in the ubiquitous media coverage that astounded the world in 1969. NASA suppressed any hint that its space travelers had to answer nature's call. Consider that the biggest laugh eight years earlier on comedian Bill Dana's top-selling 1961 live album, *Jose Jimenez—The Astronaut*, came after an interviewer down on Earth, referring to a current Soviet space craft, asked the loony Mexican astronaut, "Have you passed the Russian capsule yet?" After a long pause (which itself elicited a swell of anticipatory giggles), Jimenez answered, "Russian capsule? I never even swallowed it." NASA did not want its Apollo space program to provoke that kind of tittering hilarity.

According to David W. Woods, author of *How Apollo Flew to the Moon*, the gassy glitches didn't end with Apollo 11. Three years later, Apollo 16 commander John Young was recorded on the lunar surface via an open microphone complaining about how the vitamin-spiked orange juice and fruits designed to correct the electrolyte deficiencies of previous missions were creating a problem. "I have the farts, again," Young told fellow astronaut Charlie Duke. "I got them again, Charlie. I don't know what the hell gives them to me. Certainly not . . . I think it's acid stomach."

Duke agreed, "It probably is."

These days there are rumors from Internet sources about mysterious gas leaks on the orbiting International Space Station, including one in the Russian section that nearly caused an evacuation in September 2006, but so far nothing about UFOs (ungodly fart odors) has been corroborated. Still, given the processed diet, the weird hours, and all that weightlessness, you can be certain that those space mariners feel as gaseous as the Milky Way.

The moral is as clear as a starry night. Wherever we travel in the universe, our flatulence will follow, boldly going where no farts have gone before. We'll never reach the escape velocity to get away from them.

13

THE HORN OF PLENTY POOTING!

There hasn't been this much racket over a trumpet since Joshua ordered seven priests to blow their ram horns as they marched around the walls of Jericho.

At the 2009 semifinals of the Federation Internationale de Football Association (FIFA) World Cup games in Johannesburg, South Africa, the world's soccer fans once again had to deal with an important question: Do they sound like a horde of wasps or a herd of farting elephants? Or maybe a horde of farting wasps?

Forget the travails of attending a world-class event in a poor country where transportation is iffy and crime is rife. Visiting soccer fans complained mostly about the wailing plastic trumpets called *vuvuzelas*. Perhaps the word *trumpet* is too dignified here. The vuvuzela is a noisemaker, akin to an air horn, except it's blown like a trumpet. South African soccer fans love its tuneless blast, and nearly everyone else can't stand it—at least for now.

On June 28, 2009, *Los Angeles Times* correspondent Robyn Dixon reported: "During the current tournament, foreign players, coaches and journalists have called for a ban of the vuvuzela. There is debate about whether it's a unique part of South African culture, and therefore untouchable, or just a cheap plastic import that makes a lot of noise." When thousands of fans start blowing them at the same time, Dixon wrote, it's like "a deafening swarm of wasps. Or a herd of flatulent elephants."

To Mike Greenberg, cohost of the ESPN radio show *Mike and Mike*, "It is like you are being attacked by a swarm of locusts for ninety consecutive minutes."

Clearly, fans can't make up their minds what a vuvuzelan roar sounds like. A soccer enthusiast identified as Everton, responding to a BBC sports chat page, wrote, "This wasp-like buzzing is so irritating. Are we going to have to put up with this in the World Cup?"

Jack answered, "Yes. You will. There are many complaints [about] them, but apparently because a B-flat note is culturally significant to the people of South Africa, it's worth being allowed."

Everton: "B Flat? More like Bee Flatulence."

A writer for the Dictionary of Unfortunate Ideas explained that the "loud, annoying" vuvuzela "exactly mimics the sound effects from 1974's *Killer Bees*, starring Gloria Swanson." But other people, he added, "have described the sound as being like 'the flatulence of a billion hummingbirds' and 'a million angry Harpo Marxes.'"

Yet another correspondent described fans "blowing raspberries" on their hell horns.

Someone named Ndoda told Inside IOL, "The vuvuzela is definitely not an instrument. One note does not constitute music. Many notes blaring like they do sound more like the whole stadium farting. They are extremely irritating and I would like to see them banned. Ban the farting vuvuzelas."

An American soccer fan wrote on WorldCupBlog.org, "It still sounds like mosquitoes farting to me. . . . If the tournament was held in Singapore whoever blows one would get a good caning."

Unfortunately for vuvuzela haters, it has become such a cultural symbol for black South Africans that its banishment would create a race riot. Johnny Two Face told Inside IOL, "In Africa, we sing, dance and make noise at the stadium. If they want people to be quiet at the stadiums then why not have a 'QUIET PLEASE' sign or just tell people not to go to the stadium? If you want to watch a sport that has no celebrations . . . go watch golf or tennis. This is soccer . . . and this is Africa. . . . We going to be blowing the vuvuzela until the end."

According to the International Marketing Council of South Africa, the vuvuzela is based on kudu horns that Zulus traditionally used in their villages. On the other hand, Boogieblast, the company that imports and distributes vuvuzelas, claims on its website that they began as plastic toys from the United States and gradually started showing up at soccer games in the late 1990s. The horns range from two to three feet long and require a good set of lungs. "They're not easy to blow. You have to blow very hard," said Philip Kalinko of PerkalGifts, a Johannesburg vuvuzela distributor.

As often happens with anything that has a high annoyance factor, the vuvuzela has begun to attract a younger, international crowd of soccer rebels who'll embrace anything that pisses off a lot of people. PerkalGifts said that after the horn got so much exposure during the South African semifinals, their European orders went from almost zero to thousands a week. And seeing as FIFA has no plans to ban vuvuzelas during the 2010 World Cup finals, you can bet that fans all over the world will soon have to decide not just whether they love or hate them, but whether thousands of the horns being blasted in unison sound like a farting hive of bees, an ass-squalling swarm of wasps, a gassy herd of elephants, or the bum hums of a billion hummingbirds.

You can hear a chorus of vuvuzelas for yourself on YouTube and come up with your own description.

14

THE WORLD'S WORST FART FILM?

The list of farting scenes in Tinseltown fare, beginning with *Blazing Saddles* in 1974, is almost endless. (In my previous books I covered the history of farting in Hollywood and even spotlighted two low-budget films titled *Fart: The Movie* and *F.A.R.T. The Movie*, both of which went straight to video.) What comedy have you seen lately that *didn't* have at least one butt honk?

But if you had to pick the worst of the many films that rely on fart humor, which one would you single out as deserving of its own special Razzie Award from the Golden Raspberry Foundation?

Well, first of all, on a quality level it can't be anything like Ed Wood's non-farting *Plan Nine from Outer Space*, shot on a shoestring in the mid-fifties with nonactors, homemade special effects, and sets that shook when doors slammed. Wood's clunker classic was hobbled by a lack of talent and money. To be judged truly awful, our fart-flavored film must be a disaster of epic proportions, assembled by top-notch professionals but subverted by a combination of greed, hubris, or too many chefs in the kitchen. It must be one of those projects that looked fantastic on paper but then went horribly wrong. If there's any humor, it must be either unintentional or leaden. (It helps if the actors pause for laughs that never come.) If there are any major stars (and there should be at least one), the audience must be left to wonder, "What were they thinking?" So *Ishtar*—an empty $55-million film shot all over Morocco, starring Warren Beatty and Dustin Hoffman at $5 million each, written and directed by the gifted comedienne Elaine May—is the best example of failure I can think of. Perhaps a fart joke would have improved it. Released in 1987, *Ishtar* took one critical drubbing after another, lost $42 million at the box office when $42 million was real money, abruptly ended May's budding directorial career, and turned the meaningless word *ishtar* into a punch line for years afterward.

So what is the *Ishtar* of fart fare?

I think I've found just the film.

It's a 2002 British-German-Italian-and-who-knows-what-else production called *Thunderpants*, the aptly titled tale of an overweight eleven-year-old lad named Patrick Smash who was born with two stomachs that give him superhuman, bovine-strength flatulence. Or, as the production notes described it, his "amazing ability to break wind leads him first to fame and then to death row, before it helps him to fulfill his ambition of becoming an astronaut."

The actor who starred as Smash was neophyte Bruce Cook, whose career pretty much crashed, cratered, and burned with this movie, but his costars have fared better. Playing his best friend Alan A. Allen is Rupert Grint, now famous as Ron Weasley in the *Harry Potter* movies. Smash's sister is Anna Popplewell, who later played Susan Pevensie in the *Chronicles of Narnia* series. American character actor Ned Beatty (*Deliverance*) is a U.S. army general blessed with dialogue like "Now let's blow ass" and "You've got a heart of gold. You've got the constitution of an ox. And you've got pants . . . of thunder." Fellow Yank Paul Giamatti (*Sideways*) essays a U.S. government agent named Johnson J. Johnson.

The rest of the cast is mostly sturdy British character actors, happily gnawing on the art direction as if writer-director Peter Hewitt (formerly best known for helming *Bill and Ted's Bogus Adventure*) had removed all boundaries. Among the better known are Stephen Fry (the narrator of the *Harry Potter* films), Simon Callow (Mozart's raggedy friend in Academy

Award–winner *Amadeus*), and an uncredited Keira Knightley (*Pirates of the Caribbean, Atonement*) in a cameo as a student.

Here's the plot in a nutshell: Patrick Smash is not just born farting; his gas actually propels him like a football from his mother's womb into the arms of a doctor running toward the other side of the room. As the boy grows up, his parents must fit him with various bags and a long tube that sends his gas out the window. When he goes to school, his mates naturally treat him as a laughingstock, except for boy genius Alan A. Allen, who lacks a sense of smell. An inveterate inventor, Alan (or should I say Allen?) devises a pair of boxer shorts for Patrick (or should I say Smash?) called Thunderpants, which store and recycle his farts. After Alan comes up with a flatulence-fueled flying contraption, the U.S. Space Center sends General Sheppard (Beatty) and his agents to see what's going on. Meanwhile, the "second greatest tenor in the world" (Callow), hoping to graduate to being the first greatest tenor, hires Patrick to accompany him on tour, stand behind a curtain, and fart a high C note at just the right moment. But Smash farts at the wrong moment and causes an overhead light to fall on the world's (first) greatest tenor, standing in the wings. The poor lad is charged with murder, and thanks to a foaming-at-the-mouth prosecuting barrister (Fry), he's sentenced to death. Fortunately, just as a firing squad has taken aim and is ready to fire, Beatty's Space Center troops, led by Giamatti, drive into the prison, grab the kid—thus saving him from a fate perhaps worse than the plot of this movie—and whisk him off to America, where the film's tone changes from somber greens (the standard fart color) to bright reds. A special U.S. space program made up of genius children, ages roughly eight to thirteen, needs Smash to use his gassy powers to rescue astronauts trapped aboard an orbiting station. He emerges in the finale as a hero and literally announces the moral of the story with a bullhorn: "I'm just a nobody, really. But I did one thing right. You may think that you have problems now. Use them well. And they stop being a problem and become a gift." Oh, and did I mention the film's ponderous orchestral score, which works overtime to accompany the two-hundred-plus farts?

Several months after *Thunderpants* opened in Great Britain in May 2002, it debuted in the United States at a special fart film festival at New York City's Natural History Museum to accompany a party for the American release of an Australian children's book called *The Day My Bum Went Psycho*, by Andy Griffith. Sharing the bill were *Blazing Saddles*, *Austin Powers in Goldmember* (featuring a submarine shaped like the character Dr. Evil, with its own bubble-spurting buttocks), and the episode of HBO's *Sex and the City* in which Carrie (Sarah Jessica Parker) accidentally lets one slip in front of Mr. Big (Chris Noth) (see chapter 9). One or two celebrities, including Simon Callow, were on hand to nibble on cabbage and baked-bean hors d'oeuvres before the screening. That night turned out to be the high C note of *Thunderpants'* American presence. It would have to wait another five years before it got its U.S. premiere—on DVD.

Why did all those professionals come together to make *Thunderpants* and do it so badly? Judging from the various European entities that bankrolled it, including the British Film Council and Germany's CP Medien AG, *Thunderpants* was more of a deal than a movie, cobbled together from what seemed like disparate projects aimed at entirely different audiences. *Variety* called it "willfully eccentric" and "a single joke . . . dressed up in a lot of plot"—but overwhelmed by overambitious art direction that created an "early-'60s English Never-Never Land." The Internet Movie Database (imdb.com) proclaimed it one of the worst hundred films of all time.

But at least Paul Giamatti liked it. In an August 6, 2009, interview with Stephen Whitty of *The Star-Ledger* (nj.com), Giamatti said, "Hey, I tell you, if you like fart jokes, [*Thunderpants*] is the *Moby Dick* of fart jokes. It is the *Iliad* of fart jokes, in every conceivable variation. Actually it's the only movie my son has seen me in. He thinks that movie's genius. I think it's kind of genius, too, in its way."

Well, so was *Ishtar*, in its way. If you don't believe me, ask Elaine May. You can find her waiting at home for her agent to call back.

15

THE EARTH FARTS BACK II

In October 2002 a young scientist named Katey Walter ventured out onto the surface of a freshly frozen lake in northeastern Siberia and discovered dozens of large white bubbles of methane that had risen from the thawing permafrost at the lake's bottom only a few days earlier and gotten trapped in the ice. As soon as she cracked a small hole in a bubble with her metal hand pick, the gas came hissing up as if she had broken a pipeline. She dramatically flicked a Bic and held it above the hole. A blue flame jumped up as high as her face, nearly singeing her curly reddish hair.

Since then, the thirty-three-year-old aquatic geologist from the University of Alaska at Fairbanks has set fire to more methane "seeps" than a national champion frat-house fart burner, and some of the flames have shot as high as twenty feet. She's also lit a couple for the BBC and National Geographic TV, and there's even a video of her setting off a blue angel near Fairbanks that Al Gore screened on the floor of the U.S. Senate in late 2008. In a world filled with God's Own Peckerwoods who don't believe global warming really exists, her blunt illustration is meant to get their attention, if not their concern: Like something out of H.G. Wells, there's an enormous, backed-up, cosmic cloud of flatulence coming from the earth's distant past. It's been frozen for many thousands of years, but rising temperatures are slowly letting it rip. And like any big, obnoxious fart, people aren't going to like it.

It's like that old joke about the guy who breaks wind while he's out in the freezing cold of a winter's day. Returning to the warmth of his cabin, he shakes his foot, and a furry green ball of ice drops from the right leg of his trousers. He kicks it over toward the fireplace. The moment it hits the flames it goes "Pfffffffffffffffttt!"

Our earth is beginning to let the big pfffffffffffttt!

One of my chapters in *Blame It on the Dog* was called "The Earth Farts Back." It spotlighted recent discoveries of mind-boggling numbers of "primordial, one-celled microbes living as far down as a half-mile beneath the bottoms of the oceans" emitting "enormous amounts of [methane] gas"—enough to create "huge greenhouse bubbles" and tsunamis if let loose by earthquakes or other geological disturbances. One scientist speculated that a bubble with any more than a 5 percent mixture of oxygen and methane could create an explosive force greater than that of the world's entire stockpile of nuclear weapons.

But now geologists and climatologists are telling us that those frozen suboceanic methane pockets are *bubkes* (literally Russian for "beans", but figuratively Yiddish for "peanuts") compared to what global warming is beginning to expose beneath the Arctic landmasses, which over the past fifty years have been heating up twice as fast as the rest of the planet in what scientists call the "Arctic amplification." "Methane release due to thawing permafrost in the Arctic is a global warming wild card" capable of bringing about "abrupt changes in the climate that would likely be irreversible," Achim Steiner, head of the United Nations Environment Programme, warned in a 2008 report.

All over northern and eastern Siberia, this thaw has created thousands of shallow "thermokarst" lakes; collectively they hold fifty-five billion tons of methane that, if let loose in one big whoosh, could increase the atmospheric concentration of methane by ten times. It's already seeping up from the ground. "There's a lot of methane coming out," says Walter (who since her June 2009 marriage has expanded her name to "Katey Walter

Anthony"). "And there's a lot more to come. We call it a time bomb—but in slow motion."

She's a modern-day cross between Cassandra and Wonder Woman, determined to not only warn the world but also save it. She has spent a dozen years in northern Siberia, mastered the Russian language, earned a degree in biogeochemistry and a doctorate in aquatic biology, coauthored scientific papers and articles in such publications as *Nature, Science,* and *National Geographic,* trekked across some of the earth's most desolate topography, and dived to the bottoms of ice-cold lakes to set bubble traps that measure the amount of leaking methane. She has also worked with NASA and other agencies, studying radar imagery of permafrost areas taken from airplanes and satellites. The December 2008 issue of *Discover* magazine listed her as one of the "20 Best Brains Under 40." She's an environmental torchbearer, and she's using that torch to ignite, and illuminate, the bowels of Mother Earth.

If it seems like I'm being fatuous by comparing her displays to lighting farts, keep in mind that methane is a powerful and explosive ingredient of flatulence, whether human (roughly 7 percent), bovine, or microbial. It's not the primary element that makes your farts stink (blame that on skatol and other miniscule elements, along with sulfur), but it does help create that flame you can get if you light one. Methane is the gas that makes a swamp or a septic tank smell like the mustiest old flatus you've ever encountered. It's the gas that suffocates sewer workers and sends flames roiling through coal mines. It's unpleasant and dangerous—and never more so than when it rises into the atmosphere.

Scientists are still arguing whether methane (CH_4) or carbon dioxide (CO_2) is the more dangerous of the so-called greenhouse gases. Methane's effect in exacerbating the greenhouse problem is roughly twenty times greater than that of carbon dioxide, as it traps heat more efficiently, but methane also dissipates after a decade or so, whereas carbon dioxide can linger for more than a century. However, recent tests by NASA's Advanced

Global Atmospheric Gases Experiment program, using the latest technology, show that methane is being liberated from the Arctic five times faster than anyone previously thought. Considering that methane levels in our atmosphere have already tripled since the fossil-fuel-burning industrial age began less than two hundred years ago, that's not good news. As more methane enters the atmosphere and traps more heat, earth's mean temperature will keep rising and melt more permafrost, exposing yet more methane. It's a feedback loop, a vicious cycle that will make the earth heat up faster and faster. "I don't think it can be easily stopped unless the earth has a major cooling," says Walter Anthony.

Along with the long-buried pools and ponds of gas, the rising temperatures will expose new lakes of carbon muck. Today's microbes will begin feasting on all the thawing, rotting sabertooth tigers, wooly mammoths, steppe bison, Piltdown men, Scientology thetans, and fermenting vegetation that nature froze thousands of years ago and has kept in cold storage ever since. With nearly a quarter of the Arctic Circle's permafrost expected to be thawing by 2050, that organic matter will start sending up a veritable storm of methane and carbon dioxide to add to our woes. It could make the greenhouse gas pollution from our factories and internal combustion engines seem as inconsequential as a fart in a windstorm.

But perhaps scientists can make some lemonade out of what seems like a giant lemon. When I last heard from Katey Walter Anthony in early August 2009, she hinted that all that methane from "degrading permafrost" could actually ease the earth's looming energy shortage if we decided to harness it instead of letting it loose. "I'm working on a new project with *National Geographic* fellow explorer T. H. Culhane of Solar Cities to use (cold-loving) arctic lake microbes to improve the efficiency of biogas reactors for energy production at household and community scale," she said in an email. She was heading back out into the cold for a few months, but this time it looked like her days of lighting the earth's little one-cheek sneaks for the benefit of all those global warming deniers were over.

16

THE WORLD'S FUNNIEST FART

We all know that farts are hilarious. Why else would so many of us cackle at them like idiots and nine-year-olds? Why else would Hollywood's top film studios spend millions of dollars to elaborately set them up as punch lines?

But what is, or was, the world's funniest fart? Does such a thing exist? Is such a thing quantifiable?

If you're asking me, the answer is a simple yes, although the farts (plural) I'm championing had a lot of help to raise their funny factor. On June 9, 2008, "Will the Farter," a semiregular visitor to Howard Stern's Sirius (now Sirius XM) satellite radio show in New York, stopped by for a special segment. Like France's nineteenth-century entertainer Joseph Pujol, aka Le Petomane, Will creates flatulence on demand by anally sucking air into his lower colon and then noisily expelling it. In other words, thanks to his quirky plumbing and his control of his bellows-like abdominal muscles, Will can fart at will. And even though most of what he blasts out is not generated within his digestive tract, it can still stink fairly badly.

On this particular day, Will wanted to demonstrate his newly acquired talent as a painter, following the example of Keith Boadwee, who thirteen years earlier had created a sensation in Los Angeles by giving himself multicolored enemas and spraying them, in an abstract way, onto fifty canvases that were subsequently displayed at the famous Ace Contemporary Exhibitions

Gallery on Wilshire Boulevard. Will didn't have Boadwee's reputation as an artist to land him a gallery show, but with Stern's microphone, he didn't need it. He dipped his bare buttocks into a bowl of watercolor paint, sucked up the liquid, and spewed it onto a white canvas with a series of wet, duck-quacking farts that went on for five or six seconds at a time. He was like Jackson Pollock with Technicolor diarrhea. Howard Stern was laughing so hard he could barely speak. But the best was yet to come.

After that day's show was over, Stern sidekicks Sal Governale and Richard Christie, who record comedy bits when they're not on the air, digitally sampled Will's bubbly butt burbles and dropped them into one of their ongoing routines. The two portray a fictional morning-zoo radio team named Jack and Rod who prank people on the phone and play back the results on *The Howard Stern Show* the following day. Through a publicity service that lists second-tier writers looking for media promotion, they found Dr. Yu Chen, author of *The Voice of Medicine*, and got her "on the line" to talk about using traditional Chinese medicine to treat cancer. After a few moments of conversation, Jack and Rod told her that an in-studio guest was joining the conversation—a former cancer patient named Smokey Martling who spoke through a "cancer kazoo" embedded in his throat because part of his larynx had been removed. For the next couple of minutes Governale and Christie maintained a "dialogue" between "Smokey" and Dr. Chen by playing the watery sound effects of Will's farts. She gamely tried to grasp enough of Smokey's "questions" to provide helpful answers, even to the point of deciphering what was supposed to be Smokey's phone number. When Stern played the interview on his show the next day, everyone in the studio went into hysterics—as may you, too, if you go to youtube.com/watch?v=Kdj_dbJg-1E.

Concert hall designer and acoustics expert Trevor Cox—whom we met earlier, in chapter 4, as the man who built the world's biggest whoopee cushion—told me personally that he's never heard Will the Farter's artistic showcase, and it's probably just as well. He's more interested in analyzing the humor of the fart-like noises emanating from his extensive collection of whoopee cushions, as part of his campaign to engage young people in the science of sound. To that end, in early 2009 he launched a website, SoundsFunny.org, to find out what makes people laugh. "Listen to whoopee sounds, and vote for the funniest," he instructed his visitors. It was all *veddy* British and quite proper. The word *fart* was nowhere to be seen, because from his perch at Manchester's University of Salford, Professor Cox had a higher purpose. As he told London's *Daily Telegraph*, "For too long, acoustic engineers have concentrated on issues such as neighbor noise and concert hall acoustics; it is about time we got to the bottom of some more important fundamental issues. Really, what acoustics is about is understanding people's responses to different sounds."

The Internet news media were not as delicate. CNet News blared the headline, "Professor Launches Site to Find World's Funniest Fart!" Iwire echoed with "Searching for the World's Funniest Fart."

What inspired this search was Great Britain's Comic Relief Red Nose Day, an annual charity event that's part of National Science and Engineering Week. In preparation for the fart-tastic event, for every visitor to his Sounds Funny site, Cox played six whoopee cushion wheezes randomly selected from a total of twenty samples and asked them to grade each one from least to most laugh inducing, that is, from amusing to uproarious. "We've developed some theories about why one whoopee cushion sound is funnier than another," Cox wrote on his website, "and to test these theories we need thousands of people to cast their votes on the site before Red Nose Day." Over the following couple of weeks, thirty-four thousand curious folks from all over the world dropped by, took a listen, and made their determinations. Cox announced the results, along with sound files of the winning blurts, bleeps, and bleats in ascending order, on March 11, 2009. The poll wasn't exactly scientific, but who expects solid statistical data when you're judging rubberized fart simulations on a day named after Bozo's proboscis? Here is what he found.

1. "Longer whoopee cushion sounds are funnier." The winner was seven seconds long, "so it is better to sit on a whoopee slowly for maximum effect."

2. Visitors described three of the top five funniest whoops as being "whiny," as opposed to, say, basso profundo.

3. Women are "slightly more amused" by the wheezing of whoopees than men are. (Here I would suggest that Professor Cox's use of the word *amused* undercuts the question. Something amusing normally gets nothing more than a smile. Are women more likely to roll on the floor with laughter? I don't think so. Only we goofy guys do that.)

4. "Whoopee sounds get less funny as you get older." Well, lots of things get less funny as you get older. Maybe I should write a book.

5. "Europeans think whoopee cushions are funnier than Americans do." Maybe that's because Americans think real farts are funnier than Europeans do.

6. Whoopee cushions sound funnier "the more you listen to them." Yes, but there must be a fatigue point at which you say, "Christ, that fart *again*?"

None of this changes my conviction that Will the Farter's watery ass-whines on Howard Stern's show are the funniest ever. They were actual farts, not just the noises of air being squeezed out of glorified balloons. That's the difference between a man slipping on a banana peel and a cartoon of a man slipping on a banana peel.

In a response titled "Pffbthhhhhh!" Anna North at a women's fashion website called Jezebel suggested what perhaps could be Trevor Cox's next endeavor, now that he's found the funniest simulation of a fart: "We love watching BBC types try to analyze the humor of the whoopee cushion, but what we're really interested in is this: how do you *spell* a fart noise?"

Is it *pffffffft*?

Is it *braaaaap*?

Is it *ghumppphhh*?

The fart's in your corner, Professor Cox.

17

OUT, DAMP SPOT!

One thing that many of us know all too intimately but nobody wants to talk about is a wet fart, with its uncomfortable watery aftermath. It's the fart you can't trust, the one with lumps in it, the subversive squeaker that does more than squeak, leaving a Monster-Truck–sized skid mark on your skivvies.

But what about a damp fart, one that by definition is only moist?

The term is popping up everywhere these days as a simile for anything that's disappointing or impotent, as when a blogger recently complained that most members of the U.S. Congress are "just about as effective as a damp fart: they may stink a little, but they accomplish nothing." The term is generally matched with a positive comparative word to achieve its effect through irony; a dull person is "as charismatic as a damp fart"; someone with no sense of humor is "as hilarious as a damp fart."

What gives the damp fart such a bad name is that its humidity tends to muffle the sound, which means you not only feel an uncomfortable moisture in the seat of your pants, but you can't even brag about it. At best it merely fizzles like a wet firecracker. There's no joy or laughter in its delivery. Still, there's some confusion about the meaning of a damp fart as a figure of speech, created perhaps by the various definitions of *damp* itself. Yes, it's generally a synonym for the adjective *moist*; but it's also a noun, sometimes called "black damp," for "foul or poisonous gas that sometimes pollutes the air in coal mines"; and it's a verb, "to damp," for restricting oxygen to a fire, which is why coal and wood stoves have an adjustable plate called a damper. In blues songs the familiar "turn your damper down" means to reduce sexual ardor. This last definition makes a damp fart the equivalent of a wet blanket.

According to the *Oxford English Dictionary*, damp—or *domp*—first appeared in the late fifteenth century, in William Caxton's *The Cronicles of England*, to describe a noxious vapor: "After this dragon shal come a good and ther shal come oute of his nostrel a domp that shal betoken honger and grete deth of peple." Barnaby Googe, in his *Heresbach's Foure Bookes of Husbandry* (1577), described how "The Fennes and Marshes, in the heate of the yeere, duo send foorth pestilent and deadly dampes." By 1675 a damp was an "unwholesome draught," which almost makes the term "damp fart" a redundancy. But these days, as it pertains to farts, damp has mostly become an adjective denoting the aforementioned colonic humidity that interferes with their noise and their natural clearance of intestinal gas. There's also a general tendency for damp farts to smell worse, too, and linger.

Britain's damp fart seems to have arrived in the United States fairly late. Sure, American novelist Raymond Chandler, as early as his October 2, 1946, letter to book publicist Dale Warren, wrote "Being, like all those who have worked in Hollywood, somewhat a connoisseur of the damp fart, I place Mr. [Edmund] Wilson high on the list." But Chandler was raised and educated in England.

When artist Salvador Dali published his 1965 American autobiography, *Diary of a Genius*, he included in the early editions a reprint of a facetious nineteenth-century British booklet called *The Benefit of Farting Explain'd*, written under the pseudonym Don Fartinando "and translated into English at the Request, and for the Use of the Lady Damp-fart of Her-Fart-Shire by Obediah Fizzle, Groom of the stool to the Princess of Arsmimini in Sardinia."

But the expression owes its current popularity to the British entertainment industry. Thirty years ago, in 1980, it still had an echo of shock value when John Lydon, better known as punk rock vocalist Johnny Rotten of the Sex Pistols, told *High Times* magazine, "I had no faith in the Pistols that amounted to anything other than a damp fart." Nowadays it's just a standard put-down among music, theater, and literary critics. Reviewing the 2005 CD reissue of Patti Smith's 1975 *Horses* album, rock critic Matteo Pericoli wrote of one of its songs, "'Free Money' wheezes out of the speakers in a damp fart of treacly pianos and anemic guitars and Patti's overwrought mewling with little or no regard for tempo." In his 2007 book *State of the Union*, Michael Billington, theater critic for the *Guardian* in London, lambasted the West End's bland 1970s musicals because they "resonated with all the excitement of a damp fart." On August 1, 2008, TV critic Pat Stacey of the *Dublin Herald* described British Olympian track star Colin Jackson, subject of a BBC documentary, as "A Very Boring Man. He may be able to run like the wind but when it comes to personality, Colin is as exciting as a slow, damp fart." The blognoscenti and web posters have also joined the melee. One angry *Dr. Who* fan wrote to Digitalspy.co.uk complaining of the British TV series' newest incarnation: "I was expecting pithy humor, witty dialogue, fantastic acting and gripping storylines. Instead I got the televisual equivalent of a damp fart in a box." (For more on that, see chapter 19.) According to another post, "Not every ending of [ABC TV's] *Lost* has to have you clamping your hands to your head, exclaiming 'Fucking HELL!' But at the same time, an ending to an episode shouldn't be a damp fart, either." Damp-fart finales seem to be a common bugaboo. Stylusmagazine .com, for instance, said that director Danny Boyle's 2002 zombie flick *28 Days Later* "ended with all the potency of a damp fart."

Not even the world of video game reviews can escape the moist and muffled magumbo. A GamersDailyNews.com critic had reservations about Sega's new combat game *The Club* because "The gun blasts are guttural and meaty, while others sound like a damp fart, so the balance isn't quite there."

I'm still not sure what a damp fart is or whether I'd recognize it from its sound. All I know is that if your butt crack is feeling slightly moist, but you don't feel any lumps, you probably just let one.

18

THE VROOM IN THE ELEPHANT

If you're sitting around swapping fart jokes and funny stories, you can't go too long before somebody brings an elephant into the room. After all, if a mere human can clear a room with just one butt bomb, imagine what a creature several times larger—in fact, the largest land mammal on earth—can do. I've seen a talented raconteur get a good five minutes of material, not to mention another few minutes of laughter, from his tale of lighting an elephant's fart and nearly burning down the circus. Considering that an elephant releases enough methane in one day to drive a car twenty miles, you can get a lot of mileage out of a joke about a pachyderm's paroxysms.

Take the one about two Kenyan doctors having a debate in the corridor of a London hospital. "It's *phoom*," says one. "No, it's *phwoom*," the other insists. A helpful English doctor comes by and offers, "Gentleman, I believe the word is *womb*." The Africans shake their heads. "Sorry, but you've never really listened to an elephant break wind." Which leads us to another old joke: What's the difference between a tavern and an elephant fart? Answer: One's called a bar room, and the other goes *barrooom*! Then there's the so-called "elephant fart" that's a favorite of frat boys and other party animals after they've gone through the first couple of kegs. You put your hands behind one of your knees and hold your leg up to your chin but let the foot hang free so that your lower leg dangles like an elephant's trunk; then you either let the loudest fart in your rectal repertoire or simulate it by blowing air through your pursed lips. It promises hours of entertainment. Even your kids can join the elephantine fun with a plush toy called Norman PhartEphant that lets any one of eight different farts when you squeeze its tail.

But sometimes elephants and farts don't go together as gaily as Barnum & Bailey. Take, for example, the *Bangkok Post* headline from October 11, 2007: "Elephants Die of Flatulence!" According to the story, veterinarian Anurut Angkusing reported that two elephants named Phang Joi and Phang Grandma at the Night Safari in northern Thailand's Chiang Mai province, passed away after passing gas, "possibly from eating insecticide-contaminated grass. . . . A large amount of gas was found inside the stomachs of the elephants, both of which died on Saturday. Undigested grass may have generated too much gas." Three other elephants suffered from severe cramps, but survived.

When the zoo's grass suppliers from three nearby villages denied using pesticide or insecticide, the vets investigated more closely and found that the elephants had been fed the wrong kind of grass and got really bad indigestion. Suphoj Maythaphirat, a Night Safari senior official, said that from now on the keepers would give the elephants only soft grass, in smaller portions, along with more water.

Lest the Democrats out there laugh about the gas-bag, blow-hard elephant being the perfect symbol of the Republican Party, I should point out that the first-century Roman historian Pliny the Elder, in his *Historia Naturalis*, wrote that certain plants, including cotton thistle, made donkeys "fall a fizzling and farting." In fact, cotton thistle—the emblem of Scotland—is known scientifically as *Onopordum acanthium*; *onos* is the Greek word for donkey, and *pordum* refers to flatulence.

Chiang Mai, roughly four hundred miles north of Bangkok, is the Asian elephant capital of the world, blessed with some of the country's highest mountains and lushest tropical jungles, where the last of the large, lumbering creatures still live in dwindling numbers in the wild. There are elephant parks, conservation centers, and sanctuaries all over the area. But according to TeakDoor.com, "death in captivity has been a problem with elephants. In 2007 alone forty-seven elephants died in parks, circuses, and zoos, often for unknown reasons." Night Safari, with land that lies within the Suthep-Pui National Park, was already under scrutiny from conservationists because of poor management when its two flatulent elephants died. However, it claimed that it offers safe haven to elephants, which are mostly retired logging animals that wouldn't survive on their own because of dwindling habitat and poaching.

African elephants are likewise undergoing a stressful depopulation, but fortunately there are still plenty of happy pachyderms freely breezing in great health in select parts of the Dark Continent. South African travel writer Carol Lazar, in a piece called "Downwind of a Farting Elephant," recalled that during her stay at Botswana's Chobe National Park, "A majestic elephant bull walked directly in front of me, then paused to browse. Slowly he turned until all I could see was his rounded rump. Then he farted, a booming, thunderous *phluuut* that almost blasted me from my hammock. As I watched, his rear aperture enlarged and from it emerged a great, steaming, never-ending golden-brown turd. Then another . . . and yet another. I was mesmerised."

But really, did the elephant fart that loudly? "Yes," Lazar claimed, "because when the final dropping parted ways with its maker, he farted again, a cracking, loud, proud *phluuut* causing a flock of red-billed francolin to scatter. . . . His stomach rumbled, then, flatulating explosively, he walked towards the waterhole to join three other bulls. . . . I leapt from the hammock and wrote in my notebook: 'Almost deafened by a flatulent elephant.'"

Luckily the fart was only a *phluuut*. A *phwoom* might have been fatal to Ms. Lazar.

Let's face it, elephants are naturally funny, simply because of their absurd shape and dimensions. What other animal could fill the role of those surreal elephant jokes such as, "How do you get an elephant on top of a tree?" "Make it sit on the seed." It would be a shame if we eventually drove these mostly gentle creatures into extinction. But whatever their fate, they'll continue, in spirit, tickling our descendants on the Internet. Among seemingly countless examples, you can hear an elephant fart at Lake Manyara National Park in Tanzania at Youtube.com/watch?v=1Wd3fNXCqQc. Or you can visit a zoo elephant that farts and shits for kids at Metacafe.com/watch/1214345/elephant_shitting_and_farting.

Personally, I think it sounds more like *phoom*!

19

WHO CUT THE CHEESE?

Great Britain's most venerable science fiction TV program is *Doctor Who*, a BBC series about a time traveler (Doctor Who) in present-day England. The show ran from 1963 to 1989 and then was reactivated with a new cast in 2005. (In the United States it airs on the Syfy Channel and BBC America.) Since the show's return, it has occasionally used flatulence as humor, as when it introduced an alien race called the Slitheen that broke wind all the time, sparking at least one great line from Doctor Who (David Tennant): "Excuse me, do you mind not farting when I'm saving the world?"

But what got the U.K. buzzing was Tennant's appearance on Graham Norton's popular, very dishy BBC Two talk show in late March 2007. Doctor Who's sometimes faulty time machine is a blue, 1950s-style London bobby's call box called the TARDIS (Time and Relative Dimensions in Space), which is just as iconic to *Doctor Who* fans as the Starship *Enterprise* is to Trekkies. So when Tennant admitted to Norton that he and fellow cast member John Barrowman often sneaked into the TARDIS and farted when they knew the other actor or their female costar would be doing a scene inside, it was big news. "John is the real master . . . he can fondle out a fart like no one else," Tennant told Norton's national audience.

This set up the *possibility* of a Bud Abbott and Lou Costello moment:

"Who farted in the TARDIS?"

"Yes."

"No, Abbott, I mean, who farted in there?"

"Yes, he did."

"Wait a minute. Somebody cut the cheese in there."

"Who."

"That's what I'm asking *you*, who cut the cheese?"

"Who did."

"That's what I want to know. Who farted?

"Yes, and very loudly, too."

"Who?"

"Yes."

"Who?"

"Yes, that's the man."

"Who's the man?"

"Yes, indeed."

"Abbott, slow down. Okay, somebody farted."

"Who."

"That's what I'm asking you. Who farted?"

"Yes, he did."

"Who?"

"How many times do I have to tell you, Lou? It was Who."

"I don't know. Why are you asking me?"

But Graham Norton instead went for more sophisticated comedy by harassing passersby on the street outside his studio with a prop TARDIS and a hidden speaker that made the sounds of grunts and farts. When one poor chap went inside to investigate, a forklift picked up the TARDIS and carried him into the studio for further ridicule.

20

BOYS WILL BE BOYS

According to a recent joke, a high school stoner is going home on a crowded, noisy bus when the sausage pizza he ate for lunch begins to nag at him. The music is real loud, so he figures that if he can time several farts to the heavy beat, none of the other kids will know it's him. Lifting a cheek very slightly, he lets a few really good ones rip until he feels a whole lot better. But when he looks around, he realizes that his classmates are all looking at him funny.

"What's wrong?" he asks, removing his iPod headphones.

In real life, however, fifteen-year-old Jonathan Locke, Jr., a skinny eighth-grader at the Bill Duncan Excel Center in South Lakeland, Florida, apparently wasn't shy about farting in front of his friends on the bus. He got suspended for three days after the driver turned in the following report to the school principal: "Jonathan passes gas on the bus to make the other children laugh and it is so stink [sic] that you can't breathe after he does it."

Farting itself isn't prohibited by name, Polk County School District Special Services Director Jerome Corbett told John Chambliss of the *Lakeland Ledger*, who had been enjoying a slow news day when the call came in. (There's not even a regulation barring flatulent job titles like Polk County School District Special Services Director.) But according to Mr. Corbett, "There's a rule against disturbing the bus." If the flatulence is excessive to the point where it's creating a problem, he said, it's the bus driver's job to report it to the school administrator.

But wait a second. "It wasn't even me," Jonathan protested. "It was a kid who sits in front of me." But none of Jonathan's classmates came forward to corroborate his innocence. In effect, they threw him under the bus.

The ruckus had begun on Monday afternoon, March 16, 2009, when a nearby student started making noises with his mouth. Moments later, according to Chambliss's account, "students smelled a pungent aroma. 'I started laughing,' Jonathan said. 'It was a bad smell.'"

The next day, when Jonathan tried to get on the bus, the driver handed him the suspension form and ordered him off. Jonathan had to call his father for a ride home. The old man was plenty pissed, not at Jonathan but the administrators. "You're not going to stop a kid from laughing if it's [about] passing gas," he later told Chambliss.

It didn't help that Bill Duncan Excel Center is a last-chance school where Jonathan, who at fifteen was already too old for eighth grade, had been sent after being expelled from a regular middle school for fighting. To make matters worse, any student who gets kicked out of Bill Duncan is expelled from the district school system—much like the gas that Jonathan reportedly expelled from his butt. A teenager's life was being derailed over a few stinky farts. But what makes Jonathan's fate particularly galling is that going all the way back to Thomas Hughes's *Tom Brown's Schooldays* in the nineteenth century, farts and schoolboys have gone together like greasy eggs and diarrhea. Boys run only forward in life, grabbing excitement and experience and knowledge, burning up everything behind them like rocket fuel. Besides, where else but on the school playground did you first hear "Beans, beans, the musical fruit, the more you eat, the more you toot, the more you toot, the better you feel, beans beans for every meal"? Or "Gene, Gene, built a machine, Frank, Frank, turned the crank, Art, Art, let a fart, and blew the whole machine apart"? How else could young, uncouth lads learn to appreciate poetry?

I have more than a passing (heh heh, I said "passing," heh heh) interest in this story because I was suspended from Parkersburg High School in West Virginia for three days during my senior year in 1962, just a couple of months before graduation. Two other students and I had sat at different tables in study hall, making farting noises with the palms of our hands, taking turns drawing the teacher to different parts of the room, until some brownnoser ratted us out. Having already made plans to join the Marine Corps, I didn't care, but still, it was humiliating even for a class clown like me.

You see, Jonathan Locke's run-in with antifart fascism wasn't just an aberration. Let's move on now to the northern reaches of the American East Coast, where the Camden-Rockport Middle School (CRMS) in Camden, Maine, serves a chain of five tourist towns and fishing villages. The school sits among Victorian bed-and-breakfasts and hillside pines, looking out over Penobscot Bay. It's a postcard picture, serene enough to drive eighth-grade boys into contests to see who can let the loudest, grossest, rottenest farts. And it's orderly enough to make the local authorities penalize those boys with detention.

"Strange, but true, thanks to a bunch of 8th-grade boys, intentional farting has been banned from CRMS," said the school's weekly *Fire Cracker* newsletter in early February 2008. "It started out as a funny joke and eventually turned into a game. This is the first rule at CRMS that prevents the use of natural bodily functions. The penalty for intentional farting is a detention, so keep it to yourself!"

Holly S. Anderson, a reporter for the *Knox County Times*, blew the case wide open in her Village Soup column (knox.villagesoup.com), datelined February 4. "For adults, farting is something that we desperately try to contain and make private. This story brought me back to grammar school, when boys had the magical ability to produce farts upon demand and aim them at the people they disliked. But it is doomsday for those 'intentional' farts in Camden, ME, as they have banned it. The joke's on the boys as the penalty for 'intentional farting' is now a detention."

Seventh-grader Jordan Tyler told Anderson that the eighth-graders' escapades were well known at the school. "They would do it in science class and other places." Fellow seventh-grader Kyle Ruger said that even though farting was funny, he had "mixed feelings" about its appropriateness. But a seventh-grade girl, Jordan Knowlton, "minced no words when she expressed how she felt, saying, 'It's gross.'" (Author's note: Well, yes, but she's a *girl*.)

CRMS principal Maria Libby acknowledged that the school had rules against "disruptive behavior," but denied any official "ban on intentional farting"—thus delighting any red-blooded boy by actually saying the F-word (OK, *that* F-word) on the record. When was the last time you heard *your* school principal say "fart" for the local paper? Libby told Anderson that "detention is only warranted if the behavior is deemed a disruption. It's not a new policy, but farting can be considered a disruption."

Writing for *American Chronicle*, Robert Paul Reyes took more of a "guy" approach to this tempest in a chamber pot. "I'm not surprised that middle school boys have refined farting into a game. It would take a severe behavior modification program to stop boys from engaging in such tomfoolery." He was firmly against putting them on detention "for behavior that is normal, albeit gross, for teenagers."

Reyes was also concerned about the presumption of guilt. "How can a teacher determine if an episode of farting is intentional? If the suspect lifts a cheek, or has a huge smile on his face when he lets loose—we can assume it's intentional. But I know an old coot who farts all the time, I suspect he does it on purpose, but he doesn't give himself away by smiling or any other suspicious behavior."

A legal website called US Law, in an item called "New Rule: No Farting in School," likewise questioned the evidence—and the means of punishment. "(1) If the noise emanates from a group of kids, how will the Fart Monitor know who uncorked it? (2) Will the teacher supervising the detention get time-and-a-half? A clothes pin? Hey Principal Libby, lighten up. It's just a phase!"

Indeed, and it's a phase that should soon resolve itself without any meddling from the school officials. As Reyes saw it, "The eighth-grade boys will outgrow their penchant for farting once they realize it doesn't go over very well with girls."

When I contacted Holly Anderson a year and a half later, in August 2009, she confirmed Reyes's prediction. "I believe the issue was taken care of," she said, "because we heard no more complaints about similar behavior, and since then that class has moved to the high school where hopefully more important things have captured the boys' attention."

21

THE BLAME GAME

There's an old expression that goes, "It's better to fart and bear the shame, than hold the fart and bear the pain."

But if you're going to drop a silent-but-deadly in the company of other people, why do you have to bear the shame? Why not just blame the damn thing on someone else?

George Carlin remarked back in 1996 that if two people are on an elevator and one person farts, everybody knows who did it. But once you've added a third person, you've gone from being company to a crowd, and assigning blame gets trickier. If you're the guilty person, your best bet is to remain quiet and wait for someone else to announce that a fart has been unleashed in the general vicinity—usually as a question ("All right, who farted?" or "Did somebody die?") or an exclamation ("Holy shit!" or "Whooo-eee!"). At that crucial point, blame must be aimed.

Among strangers, of course, this rule of blame will usually have the effect of convincing everyone to ignore the odor and pretend it didn't happen—and thus the passed gas will get a pass and pass away without remark. But among friends or acquaintances, such a stinky invasion of privacy can't go unannounced.

That's why we have the blame game. No, it's not a Shirley Ellis oldie. There's no "Blame, blame, bo bame, banana fana fo fame, fee fi mo mame, *blame.*" You simply wait for someone to react to the sudden atmospheric disturbance and then you deliver a modern equivalent of that old saw, "A fox smells his own hole first"—which means that if someone accuses you of something, they probably did it themselves. Only now, in the age of hip-hop, you have to put it into a rhyme, the most basic being, "You said it, you let it." Someone else can then try to answer your rhyme with a better one. It's like playing the dozens ("Yo' mama so stinky they named a fart after her!"), only you attack the person next to you instead of insulting his (or her) mother. Creativity deflects the pointed finger and blames *it* as the one that was figuratively pulled.

Here are a few:

"The smeller's the feller."
"You smelt it, you dealt it."
"You denied it, you supplied it."
"You named it, you claimed it."
"You observed it, you served it."
"You detected it, you ejected it."
"You announced it, you bounced it."
"He who speaks is the one who reeks."
"You said the rhyme, you did the crime."
"You spoke fast, you set off the blast."
"You tried to save face, you stunk up the place."
"You waved your hand, it came out of your can."
"You shouted 'Pee-yew,' so it must be you."
"You pooh-poohed it, you dood it."

Try it yourself: if you made the best verse, maybe you made the atmosphere worse.

22

BREAKING NEWS: TIGER TEES OFF!

The clip was everywhere on the Internet on August 3, 2009, from YouTube (very briefly) on down to a few dozen duffers' blogs. Taken just a day earlier, on Sunday, the video was a live CBS telecast of golfing sensation Tiger Woods sizing up an approach shot on the eighteenth fairway at Warwick Hills in Grand Blanc, Michigan. Woods was securely in the lead with three strokes at the PGA Buick Open, so the announcers in their soft voice-overs were trying to liven up what was otherwise a static moment: "He's gonna try to let it release a little bit more," one of them murmured. A second voice chimed in: "Tiger waits."

Suddenly, as if following their instructions, Woods swung his right foot backward and—*brrrrraaapp*! It released all right. Apparently some hidden, sensitive microphone heard it loud and clear, a real trouser rouser, not just a one-putt. Tiger and his caddy, Steve Williams, looked at each other and broke out laughing.

The *Chicago Sun-Times* sliced right to the heart of the matter in its next-day headline: "Does a Tiger Fart in the Woods?"

Or did the caddy do it?

And why was it so damn loud?

The PGA and CBS-TV added to the mystery of whodunit, or whether it was really done at all, by demanding that YouTube pull down the fairway fart flick that had popped up within hours of the deed—leaving only a black square hole where the action had been. "If it was Tiger that let one rip before he let one rip, it makes him a human being. If it wasn't Tiger, same thing," NBC commentator Josh Alper wrote later in the day. "By taking out the oversize eraser, though, the PGA makes it seem like something serious and heinous happened instead. That's just dumb, although the fact that it will only make more people search for the video makes it all worthwhile." The popular gossip site TMZ took up the slack by posting the video prominently, along with the headline "FartGate" and the question, "Take a close look at Tiger's reaction—is that the face of a guilty, gassy man?" Keith Olbermann aired it and asked basically the same question on his MSNBC *Countdown* show.

The *Detroit Free Press* headline asked, "Was Tiger Woods a Bit Too Gassed Up for Buick Open?" and subheaded it with Rodney Dangerfield's famous quote from the golf comedy *Caddyshack*: "Whoa, did somebody step on a duck?"

"It happens," said the article. "And when Tiger Woods is a suspect, it ends up on YouTube. Isn't celebrity great?"

USA Today remarked on how quickly the wind broke mainstream and went viral: "The most searched-for video on Google on Monday was 'Tiger Woods fart,' while the same search term jumped to nine on the Google Trends list. The video undoubtedly would have been among the most viewed on YouTube had the PGA Tour not chosen to take the clip down on the grounds of copyright infringement." The national newspaper also introduced evidence that Tiger had at least one prior: "This is not the first video alleging Tiger flatulence. A 2006 YouTube clip claiming to capture Woods passing gas has more than 1.4 million views."

But Ty Votaw, executive vice president of communications for the PGA Tour, quickly stepped in to declare the golf superstar's innocence. "I can confirm after consultation with CBS it was not Tiger Woods," he told *USA Today*. TMZ instantly updated its story with the headline: "FartGate— CBS Denies Tiger Supplied It!"

By the next day, Tuesday, the real story was starting to leak out. Mike Brody at MyFox National reported, "The *Examiner*[.com] says it was a practical joke played by someone in the gallery with a whoopi [sic] cushion, and Fox Sports is blaming the gas attack on mischievous CBS announcer David Feherty."

Randy Youngman of the *Orange County Register* in Southern California agreed, telling Dashiell Bennett of Deadspin.com, "A few years ago, I interviewed Feherty before the Toshiba Classic at Newport Beach Country Club, and he confessed that he, Woods, and Tiger's caddy, Steve Williams, sometimes have off-camera farting contests during tournaments. 'If you see Tiger and Stevie laughing hysterically (on camera) and you can't figure out why,' Feherty told me, 'it might be because one of them loudly passed gas.'"

Detroit Free Press sportswriter James Jahnke seconded Youngman: "The Web has whirred with theories and accusations regarding the gassy culprit. Do we now have our man? [The rumor that David Feherty did it] is far from official, but it wouldn't shock us. After all, we figured it was Feherty two days ago."

Feherty played coy, however. According to Sports Illustrated.cnn.com, "Feherty informed us [the fart] came from the gallery. Credit Feherty for solving the mystery."

But other observers, including Totalprosports.com in an August 5 item called "Tiger Woods Fart Mystery Solved; David Feherty Cut the Cheese," insisted that Feherty—a Northern Ireland-born former golf pro whose very name, especially when spoken by an Irishman, almost indicts him—was indeed the culprit. "[A] source who has chosen to remain anonymous is indicating that it was CBS golf analyst David Feherty. Whether he produced the noise with the power of his own ass, or needed the assistance of some electronic device is unknown, but the source has also stated that the Tiger and Feherty have been engaged in a fart contest with each other for some time now."

Feherty—a notorious prankster who had been standing only a few yards away from Tiger, just out of camera range, when the fart occurred—

was certainly a likely candidate. He's a loose cannon in what is normally regarded as a gentleman's game. When Scientologist-actor Tom Cruise asserted on a talk show that physical exercise, not therapy or drugs, was the best cure for depression, the depressive Feherty told *Golf* magazine, "If I kicked the shit out of Tom Cruise, I'd feel a lot better about myself." And in May 2009, less than three months before the Tiger flap, Feherty flashed his goober credentials when he wrote in *Dallas* magazine that if a returning Army vet from Iraq found himself in an elevator with a rifle, two bullets, House Speaker Nancy Pelosi, Senate Majority Leader Henry Reid, and Osama Bin Laden, "there's a good chance that Nancy Pelosi would get shot twice." This was not your average preppy play-by-play guy.

Some investigative mavens were studying the fart's acoustics in hopes they would lead to the perpetrator. The *Chicago Sun-Times'* Dan Cahill said the rumors that Feherty was using an electronic device, possibly an iPhone with a fart app, made sense. "It explains the artificial sound and the perfect timing. It also explains why Tiger—who will go berserk if a bird flies over during his backswing—laughed it off."

Detroit's popular WRIF-FM morning zookeepers Drew Lane and Mike Clark added to the chorus by replaying Tiger's post-match interview on their program with lots of overdubbed farts punctuating Tiger's innocent lines, including, "I did over-cut that [shot] into the wind"—*brraaaap!*

Dashiell Bennett at Deadspin.com may have gotten in the last word when he dubbed the brouhaha "The Dumbest Sports 'Scandal' of the Year," saying, "The saddest part, of course, is that it was completely obvious from the very beginning that Woods was never the culprit. I'm not even sure that anyone farted. It sounds more like a movie sound-effect fart. . . . The fact that I've spent this much time trying to figure out the source of the raspberry makes me question my choice of careers a little bit."

Unfortunately for Tiger Woods, all this speculation and bombast was just a warm-up for "The Biggest Sports Scandal of the Year," which broke almost four months later, after a late-night car crash led to speculations about his angry wife chasing him out of his Florida mansion on Thanksgiving Night with a 2-iron. Subsequent revelations about his dalliances—with Las Vegas cocktail waitresses, strippers, hookers, and porn stars—almost overnight wrecked his billion-dollar image, if not his golfing career, and ended the world's greatest commercial endorsement empire, indicting not so much Tiger's natural weakness for hoochie-mamas but rather the hypocrisy of the bloated golf cartel.

Like JFK's assassination, Tiger's who-farted whodunit will probably remain a mystery. Perhaps in years to come, conspiracy theorists will still be debating the question of where the shot came from on that gassy knoll.

23

THEY HAVE A LITTLE ODOR

Emily Dickinson was a recluse who died in her parents' comfortable Amherst, Massachusetts, home where she had been born fifty-six years earlier. She spent her last decades in a bedroom, and by the late 1860s she would talk only through a door, though she often wrote notes and letters to old friends and sent little gifts to folks around town. One man who saw her in 1870, when she was forty, described Emily as "a plain little woman with two smooth bands of reddish hair." Only one known photograph of her, an 1847 daguerreotype of an innocent teenager, exists; a later photo from the 1850s is in dispute. Her neighbors naturally wondered what she did in that house all day and night, especially after her parents died.

Nobody knew that Emily was crafting tight little poems. Fewer than a dozen of them, published anonymously, made it into print during her lifetime. Only after she died in 1886 did her younger sister, Lavinia, discover that Emily had written nearly eighteen hundred of them—along with instructions that they all be burned. They were quirky little capsules of observation, mostly a few lines each, with slant rhyme, eccentric meters, and unconventional capitalization and punctuation. Emily hadn't even given them titles. But four years later, rather than burn them, Lavinia interested a publisher in releasing the first book of Emily Dickinson's work. By the 1950s this Victorian spinster would be recognized as one of America's greatest poets.

Still, her stuff seemed strictly for girls. All you had to do was look at her first lines, which also doubled as the titles: "A bird came down the walk"; "A drop fell on the apple tree"; "I cannot dance upon my toes"; "Partake as doth the bee"; "Will there really be a morning?" Never mind that upon closer inspection many of these poesies were musings about death, sorrow, and immortality. For example, "Will there really be a morning?" is about one of those long, sleepless nights of the soul when things are so dark, so bleak, that sunrise seems impossibly far away.

And I have a suspicion, shared by nobody else, that Emily may also have penned an ode to farts.

Oh, you don't believe me? It's called "They Have a Little Odor" and it even has a number, 785, that a Dickinson scholar assigned to it about sixty years ago. The poem goes like this:

> They have a little Odor—that to me
> Is metre—nay—'tis melody—
> And spiciest at fading—indicate—
> A Habit—of a Laureate—

Judy Jo Small, who wrote a 1990 book called *Positive as Sound: Emily Dickinson's Rhyme*, would never even think of reading such a disgusting thing into that poem. According to her, "That Jim Dawson is a sick, *sick* individual!" Well, no, I'm kidding. What she actually said was, "Dickinson determined to write poetry that would escape definition, like music, like an elusive fragrance. . . . The word 'Laureate' here involves a pun on the plant name *Laurus nobilis*, the bay laurel, of which the aromatic leaves are spicier when fried. Laurels, traditionally used for wreaths of honor, the verse also suggests, belong to the poetic 'melody' that fades beautifully." If Small were here right now, she'd probably pull out, as Exhibit B, an 1864 letter that Dickinson wrote to sisters Louisa and Fannie Norcross rhapsodizing about her "garden off the dining-room," wondering "Would it interest the children to know that . . . we have primroses, like the little pattern sent in last winter's note, and heliotrope by the aprons full—the mountain colored one—and a jasmine bud, you know the little odor like Lubin—and gilliflowers, magenta, and a few mignonette, and sweet alyssum bountiful, and carnation buds?"

Okay, but so what? Here's how Professor Dawson, late of the West Virginia University English Department, might interpret it.

They have a little Odor [*so far so good*]—that to me

Is metre—nay—'tis melody—[*they come in bursts, but with each note different enough to suggest a lilting tune*]

And spiciest at fading [*and how! my nose hairs are curling!*]—indicate—

A Habit—of a Laureate—[*forget the wreath; you know how those poet laureates are, going hours without food in their garrets as they torture themselves over each line, nursing rumbling stomachs and bad digestion, feeling that each gassy pang is a blessed recrimination, nay, a badge of honor within the poet's guild, e'er a plangent obligation*]

Convinced?

Okay, here are a few more exhibits of Emily's poems, such as "There came a wind like a bugle" and "A clock stopped"—the latter a reference to those really stinky ones that evince such responses as, "Whooo, that one could stop a goddamn clock!" And then of course there's "A darting fear—a pomp—a tear," which to my jaded ear is Emily playing with a spoonerism; yes, I'm saying that what she really means is "A farting dear—a poop [*an old word for a fart or an elderly man, and Emily loved archaic words*]—a tear [*which can also rhyme with air, as in the "rip" of a good one*]." Could this be her father sitting in his study, stinking up the place, or an imagined lover with a gas problem?

Don't believe me?

A darting fear—a pomp—a tear—
A waking on a morn
To find that what one waked for,
Inhales the different dawn.

Let's go back to "There came a wind like a bugle":

There came a wind like a bugle; [*nudge nudge*]

It quivered through the grass, [*oh, I'll bet it did*]

And a green chill upon the heat [*farts are green*]

So ominous did pass [*she said "pass," heh heh, like* gas, *heh heh*]

We barred the windows and the doors [*Katy bar the door, here comes a big one!*]

As from an emerald ghost; [*emeralds are green, farts are green, need I say more?*]

There's more, but it doesn't fit my thesis, so I'll just pretend it doesn't exist.

Ah yes, I'm in love with a wonderful girl. Sure, she's been dead for more than a century, but it's so romantic to dream about her sitting there in her lonely room, forsaking the corset in order to let her inner world go free, rhapsodizing under the soft glow of an oil lamp about letting dainty little stinky ones slip from her bustle-less bottom.

Yes, they have a little odor indeed.

24

CREPITATION WITHOUT REPRESENTATION!

Nobody ever accused Iowa Republican Senator Charles E. Grassley of being ahead of the curve, but he was certainly onto something back in 1990 when he facetiously suggested that cattle, notorious for expelling large amounts of methane from both ends, should be fitted with airbags, complete with catalytic converters, to harness their nether exhalations. "And if that doesn't work in reducing cow methane gas emissions," said the soybean farmer-politico, "we can tax them. Call it another gas tax."

Little did he know.

By the beginning of the twenty-first century, people all over the world were talking about the increase of yet another so-called greenhouse gas—carbon dioxide—and its deleterious effect on the earth's atmosphere. As if poor old Elsie weren't already being demonized enough for spewing twenty-eight to thirty-five cubic feet of methane each day, scientists began to worry about how her cud-chewing and wind-breaking were emitting clouds of CO_2, making her an ever greater threat to the world than Grassley had predicted more than a decade earlier.

In 2003, New Zealand, an agricultural country, responded to this threat by proposing a "fart and belch" tax on its cattle and sheep farmers to raise roughly $5 million a year for research into mitigating its contribution to global warming. As I described in *Blame It on the Dog*, the Federated Farmers of New Zealand quickly nipped that idea in the bud by driving their tractors into Wellington and staging a demonstration called Fight Against Ridiculous Taxes (FART) on the steps of Parliament.

But then, five years later, in May 2008, Estonia announced its own levy on cattle—not a proposal but a de facto new tax—inspiring a near-hysteric Matt Drudge, on his popular right-wing Drudge Report website, to headline the story "Estonia Will Tax Cow Farts!" Denmark proposed its own toot tariff the following February.

And now, like an errant cow on the back forty, the idea of a gas tax has lumbered back home, not to Grassley's Iowa but to grassy, gassy Ohio, the state next door. It all came about because, on April 17, 2009, the newly Democratic-controlled U.S. Environmental Protection Agency brought into law the national Clean Air Act, which recognized an earlier U.S. Supreme Court decision, *Massachusetts vs. EPA*, that classified greenhouse gases, including those from farm animals, as pollutants. Corporation-hugging Republicans all over America, including Grassley, freaked out, but nowhere more than in Ohio, a reliably pro-business state. The old bugaboo of Washington intruding on states' rights had reared its ugly, big-government head, and something had to be done, pronto.

According to Marc Kovac, a Columbus-based reporter for several Ohio newspapers, "State lawmakers took a pre-emptive strike Wednesday [May 6, 2009] against a potential federal tax on livestock flatulence." In a symbolic declaration of Ohio's sovereignty, the state senate, on a 30-2 vote, adopted "a resolution urging federal officials to refrain from plans to charge fees to farmers for livestock emissions." Republican senators Bob Gibbs and Tim Grendell, the resolution's sponsors, claimed that the Clean Air Act could require farmers to buy fart permits "ranging from $22 to $175 per head" if they owned more than twenty-five dairy cows, fifty beef cattle, or two hundred hogs or sheep. "I think it's important to remember that when the Clean Air Act was instituted, the intent of Congress at the time was to clean up our air from smokestack industries," Gibbs told Kovac. "I don't think anyone envisioned that it would affect livestock production." Furthermore, he was convinced that a tax on cattle flatulence would be punitive and have no effect on reducing global warming. "There's not any known technology to capture the emissions from beef cows, dairy cows or hogs," he said.

This resolution didn't just materialize out of thin (but choking) air. One of Ohio's U.S. representatives, House Minority Leader John Boehner, was already fulminating against the "theory" of global warming (not to mention the theories of evolution, Elvis's death, President Obama's American birth certificate, and an orb-shaped earth). If carbon dioxide is so bad, Boehner reasoned, why did God in His wisdom create super-gassy cows in the first place? During an April 19, 2009, appearance on ABC-TV's *This Week*, Boehner told host George Stephanopoulos that cattle eructation and flatulence put CO_2 into the air all the time and have nothing to do with any perceived climate change. "The idea that carbon dioxide is . . . harmful to our environment is almost comical," he said. "Every time we exhale, we exhale carbon dioxide. Every cow in the world, you know, when they do what they do, you've got more carbon dioxide."

PoliticsDaily.com, in an article titled "Minority Leader Boehner Cites Cow Farts as Justification for His Environmental Negligence," compared the U.S. congressman's comments to an earlier oil industry ad that said "carbon dioxide was getting a bad rap in the press and that it would be un-American to implicate a gas that comes 'out of a little girl's mouth as she blows dandelions.'" The writer speculated that "windbag politicians spouting talking points on the Sunday talk shows" posed an even greater threat of "airborne CO_2," and that Boehner alone "caused an Antarctic iceberg the size of Rhode Island to fall into the ocean."

On June 2, U.S. Representative James Sensenbrenner from Wisconsin spoke out against the EPA regulations at the Heartland Institute's Third International Conference on Climate Change in Washington, D.C., saying, "To show you how ridiculous this is getting, the EPA has got the proposed regulation imposing a cow fart tax of $175 a year on every head of dairy cattle in the United States and $80 for beef cattle, $20 per head of hogs. I don't know if we're supposed to develop the technology to strap a catalytic converter on the back of a cow."

His speech prompted conservative political consultant Anthony Del Pellegrino, blogging for NJVoices, to ask, "Did you ever think you would hear a Congressman come before a national audience and talk about cow farts?" But Del Pellegrino did agree with Sensenbrenner that taxing farm animals would put many farmers out of business. "And what exactly will all the proceeds from this new tax do for curtailing greenhouse emissions? Unless it is meant to kill the cattle, milk and pork industries, I do not see what the EPA will invest this money into in order to save the environment from profuse farting. Do they intend to purchase butt plugs for pigs and cows?"

Del Pellegrino further wondered, "[H]ow far will they go if this fart tax passes? Will it not be expanded to human beings? I know a lot of people who are filled with a lot more than hot air and a per-fart price tag on them alone would reduce the deficit by millions. So how much money do you think the federal government can make by taxing all humans for their own gassy anal emissions? . . . Start saving up now for the inevitable and get used to the federal government's newest war . . . the war on farts."

25

WHO SAID FARTS ARE GREEN?

A fart ain't just a fart anymore. It's a greenhouse gas emission, which means that even though cartoonists and comedy filmmakers usually show flatulence as being a green cloud, it's not "green" environmentally.

Thanks to new cap-and-trade policies designed to deal with the world's growing global warming problem, several governments in the so-called developed world have set up carbon markets, complete with offsets to credit fossil-fuel-burning industries for maintaining sanctuary forests that consume, through photosynthesis, an amount of carbon dioxide equal to or greater than what their smokestacks cough into the atmosphere. For example, if your coal-burning factory annually exhales a billion metric tons of CO_2, you can avoid environmental restrictions and fines by funding a rain forest in Brazil or a stretch of boondocks in Appalachia that inhales an equivalent amount; and if your forests inhale more CO_2 than your factories exhale, you get carbon credits from a mitigation bank that you can trade or sell to another industry that pollutes worse than you do. It's a win-win situation for everybody, except for the environment and, ultimately, its inhabitants.

And now, according to *National Geographic News*, a Sydney, Australia-based company called Easy Being Green is selling offset credits to folks who either expel too much greenhouse gas—methane and carbon dioxide—or have pets that do so. In other words, if you and your fat Persian cat are sitting around the house blowing hisses all day, you can cancel out your environmental damage (that is, reduce your "fart footprint") and, by achieving "carbon neutrality," live guilt-free for a year simply by buying a "flatulence card" for each one of you. Think of it as an indulgence, like one of those "get out of purgatory free" blessings the Church used to sell to medieval peasants. The cost for you is about $8 American ($20 Australian). Your feline's fart card is only $6, because he's not quite as blustery as you are, unless you're feeding him Chinese cat food from the 99-Cents store.

Company spokesman Murray Hogarth told *National Geographic News* that, yeah, the fart cards are "gimmicky," but they spotlight Easy Being Green's other, more serious efforts to help consumers and small businesses offset their emissions. The company's website claims that its various products, including the flatulence card, have "reduced 620,000 [tons] of CO_2 pollution per year, the equivalent to taking 150,000 cars off the road."

Your average human gas bag lets one rip eight to fifteen times a day, expelling a total of roughly a quart of gas, and carbon dioxide composes roughly 9 percent of all that fart activity. (Nitrogen and hydrogen together compose 80 percent, but they're not considered a threat to the environment right now. And though most of us believe that methane is the greater villain, it's less than 7 percent of your butt blurt; that's why your farts flare up only slightly and turn blue when you light them with a match, instead of launching you face-first into a wall.)

Keep in mind, you and the cat are not going to stink any less, and your chronic farting is not going to become a social asset. But Easy Being Green will spend your offset money on energy-saving products like compact fluorescent light bulbs that reduce society's electrical use—very important in Australia, where most electricity comes from coal-fired plants—and make you feel noble because you're helping the environment, despite all that pollution coming out of your big fat butt. In 2006, for example, the company claimed it imported three million such light bulbs and either sold or gave them away to consumers. "In exchange," said *National Geographic News*, "customers signed over the projected carbon savings to Easy Being Green, which then sold them as carbon emission rights on the New South Wales carbon-trading market."

A front page article of the *Australian* recounted how Easy Being Green turned Jenny Cracknell into a "carbon-neutral granny" after her daughter, Emily, gave her a gift certificate to offset two years' worth of one-cheek sneaks and no-cheek boomers. "I don't like to brag, but I actually don't have much flatulence," Mrs. Cracknell said. "But when I do, I feel okay about it, because the damage to the planet has been offset."

But environmental blogger Jennifer Marohasy sees these offsets as nothing more than a feel-good solution to the problem. "It seems a rather Catholic approach; the idea that it's OK to do something as long as you pay some sort of penance and in this way [are] pardoned. That's what it's really all about, isn't it? That you can buy the right to fart?" Ms. Marohasy suggested that maybe the government should just ban foods more likely to give a person gas. Or better yet: "Maybe we should just ban capitalism. It has after all created the wealth to support a large intellectual class with nothing better to do than count the number of times its members fart."

Hey, didn't Karl Marx say that first?

26

CAN-CAN MAN WITH THE SINGING CAN!

When *Can-Can*—a salute to the high-kicking showgirls of 1890s Paris—began its two-year run on Broadway in 1953, skimpily clad mademoiselles in silk stockings were as scandalous as New York's authorities would allow. Had they trotted out the Moulin Rouge's most legendary performer—Le Petomane, a man with a trap door in the seat of his pants who could mimic birds and musical instruments with his derriere—the NYPD would have canned *Can-Can* on opening night.

As it turned out, the original audiences didn't care that the musical omitted the *fin de siecle farteur*. *Can-Can* had legs—892 performances at the Shubert Theater before the curtain dropped in mid-1955, and 394 performances in London's West End. Actress-dancer Gwen Verdon and choreographer Michael Kidd won Tony Awards. Two of the play's songs, "I Love Paris" and "C'est Magnifique," were chart singles.

But theater critics generally panned everything about *Can-Can* except the dancing and the overall *joie de vivre*. The *New York Times*, in a May 17, 1953, review said, "Cole Porter's score is not one of his best works, and Abe Burrows' book is old-fashioned and pedestrian." Though the play took place in France's Gay Nineties, it seemed trapped in the Innocent American Fifties. At the end of the decade, when Hollywood mounted *Can-Can* as an overstuffed, six-million-dollar production starring Frank Sinatra as a

French magistrate with a New Joisey accent, not even its denunciation by Soviet premier Nikita Khrushchev as "Western decadence" could raise its hip factor. Broadway's 1981 attempt to revive *Can-Can* lasted only five performances. When London producers resuscitated it seven years later with a few extra Cole Porter songs from other musicals, the play was written off as a musty artifact; it petered out after several months.

But let's go back to Khrushchev for a moment. During his famous U.S. tour in September 1959, he visited the set of *Can-Can* on 20th Century Fox's back lot and watched Shirley MacLaine, Juliet Prowse, and other scantily dressed chorines kick the can-can. Afterward, he likened all the bare thighs, long legs, and swishing bottoms to capitalist running-dog porn. He told reporters, "Mankind's face is more beautiful than its backside."

Hmmm. Since part of the original can-can routine entailed the girls turning their tushes to the audience, bending over with their hands on their knees and shaking a little tail feather, maybe what the play needed was *more* backside, *more* decadence, *more* of whatever offended a prudish old Bolshevik like Nikita Khrushchev. But many more years would pass before anyone took that idea to its inevitable, and logical, conclusion.

Finally, in 2007, a couple of California playwrights, Joel Fields and David Lee, decided it was time to give Broadway's creaky old Golden Age warhorse one more chance. Cole Porter and Abe Burrows were long dead, so they went to Burrows' TV-writer son, James, to get permission to rework the book. A comedic facelift was right up David Lee's alley; he had plenty of experience writing for television sitcoms, namely *Cheers* and *Frazier*, the latter of which he also cocreated. An aficionado of musical theater, he had already pulled a couple of oldies out of mothballs, including the obscure *Do I Hear a Waltz?* So now he was amusing himself with reimagining *Can-Can* and downsizing its dance troupe. Lee told *Playbill*'s Ernio Hernandez, "we added a few characters of our own that were actual performers at the Moulin Rouge. And of course Burrows' original premise—that of a judge and a chanteuse finding their romantic way through the demimonde of

Paris in 1893—is still at its center. Rather than a 'rewriting' of the show, Joel and I like to think of this version as a 'resetting'—as you might an outdated piece of jewelry—polishing up the gems Porter and Burrows left us." Thinking of the play's early number, "Maidens Typically of France"— with its lyric "We all go to church, we all say our prayers, and if, when we dance, we show our derrieres, it is to show that, even when we dance, we are maidens"—Lee asked himself, why not add that one historical personage who truly did present his posterior onstage? That would be Joseph Pujol, better known as Le Petomane (Fart Mania).

I've already told the story of Le Petomane in his own *Who Cut the Cheese?* chapter and chronicled his various film bios in *Blame It on the Dog.* He is the patron saint of farting, the super entertainer whose career, though successful, was always behind him. In the mid-1890s he packed the outdoor stage of the Moulin Rouge in Paris's swinging Montmartre district, singing songs and imitating musical instruments and blowing darts across the stage—all with his talented *tuchus.* Unfortunately, he began to think that he was bigger than the Moulin Rouge and that he should be his own impresario in his own theater, ultimately proving that when it came to show business, Le Petomane didn't know his ass from a hole in the ground. He eventually shut the trap door in his trousers, left behind the art of letting air biscuits, and became a thriving baker. He died in 1945.

What may have inspired David Lee to include Le Petomane was the fart man's fleeting appearance—by Australian character actor Keith Robinson— in director Baz Luhrmann's 2001 extravaganza *Moulin Rouge,* starring Nicole Kidman. Did I say fleeting? How about almost left on the cutting (cheese) room floor? If you blinked, you missed him. But Lee had greater things in mind for Le Petomane in his new *Can-Can* incarnation.

"My role [as Le Petomane] wasn't large but it was pivotal," Robert Yacko, a middle-aged Los Angeles-based theater actor, told me in September 2009. "David created him as [the female club owner] Pistache's confidante and tarot reader, so he had some of the best lines. He was always elegantly dressed and elegantly wry." Madam Pistache introduced Le Petomane, along with the other characters, in the long opening number, "Montmartre," which is the only time he demonstrated his unique stage act. "The chorus girls brought me out right after they sang 'Maidens Typically of France.' I was dressed just like you see in the old photos—sparrow coat, mustache and all. First I used a funnel, then I blew out a [trick] candle, and then I replaced the funnel with a piccolo and played it as I marched around the stage. During one verse I even sang along with my farts." The sound effects, he said, came from the orchestra pit. The trombone player used his mouthpiece rigged with a rubber extension to blow the razzers, and the piccolo player did the piccolo honors. Yacko, a trained dancer, subtly used his body to show Le Petomane's efforts to blow his own horn. "I knew how to act like I was farting without being too obvious or vulgar about it."

The musical theater veteran said he had no more than "a mild knowledge" of who Le Petomane was before he landed the role, "and then I read the book [*Le Petomane*, by Jean Nohain and F. Caradec]. During rehearsals the cast was also passing your book [*Who Cut the Cheese?*] around, and I think I really got to know and appreciate him. He was always elegant in a very theatrical way, as a counterpoint to what he did onstage, so he was the perfect character, really. David [Lee] did a great job with him."

Can-Can opened for a month's run at the fabled Pasadena Playhouse on July 9, 2007, got held over for two extra weeks, and received generally good reviews. In other words, Le Petomane, not the critics, did most of the fuming. The *Hollywood Reporter*'s Jay Reinger liked the "clever rewrite," "inspired staging," and the "choreography [which] is right up there with the best of Broadway." The lead actors were "terrific"—and way down at the end of the review, worthy of comment, was "Robert Yacko as Le Petomane, the noted French flatulist—or 'fartiste' as he's called here (with a megaphone attached to his ass)."

Entertainment Today's Travis Michael Holder called Le Petomane a "great character ... here featuring a hilariously underplayed Robert Yacko as the real-life and highly successful "fart-iste" of the era who could actually perform tunes by breaking wind into a tube leading from his ... er ... derriere, to be quite French about it. As much Mexican food as I consume, it's led me to wonder if I might seek a new career path myself this late in my life." Brad Auerbach, another *Entertainment Today* critic, felt that Yacko played the role "with aplomb" and praised the "clever breaking down of the fourth wall, [as] Le Petomane solicits from the audience at intermission a series of words ... that rhyme with can."

Los Angeles Times critic Charles McNulty was also sympathetic. "Robert Yacko manages to scrape through with his comic dignity intact as Le Petomane." And Paul Hodgins of the *Orange County Register* raved that Yacko "brings a Tony Randall-like wryness to Le Petomane."

Of course there had to be someone—in this case, Laura Hitchcock of *Curtain Up*—who wasn't enamored of the character. She said "the addition of Le Petomane, famous for farting on key, is not a real asset," and felt it was an "unnecessary role," even though "Robert Yacko shows a subtle flair for comedy."

Over the past two years, David Lee has reworked his *Can-Can* script and hopes that someday it will return to the stage. Who knows—Hollywood may even want to film it. If so, the amiable song-and-dance-man Robert Yacko better watch out, because Johnny Depp, on record as saying he wants to be Le Petomane, will be gunning for his part. "That's a role I'd do in a minute," Depp told *Playboy* back in 1996.

27

HALITOSIS HYPED AS HIPPO HOT AIR

A couple of years ago a reader asked Yahoo! Answers if hippopotamuses fart through their mouths. Someone else asked ChaCha Answers roughly the same question: "Does a hippo fart out of its mouth?"

Meanwhile, an Internet clearinghouse of weird bits of information (wernersplace.com/uselessfacts.htm) claimed in item number 405: "The hippopotamus farts through its mouth. Methane gas is released, making it notably different from a burp."

At Snopes.com, a website dedicated to debunking urban legends and other misinformation, a "Mr. Billion" wrote, "Don't ask how this came up, but my brother-in-law says that hippopotamuses (hippopotami?) expel gaseous byproducts through their mouths. He says he got this from the movie *The Ghost and the Darkness* with Val Kilmer and Michael Douglas." (He was referring to a scene near the beginning of the film in which Kilmer's character tells a stranger on a train that hippos "fart through their mouths. But they don't kiss very much.") Mr. Billion wanted to know, "Is that true?"

I suppose I could answer the question pithily enough, but Michelle—a Yahoo! Answers contributor who was probably wearing hip boots at the time—came up with the obvious: "Wouldn't 'farting through your mouth' be burping? And I know nothing about hippos."

Where do these myths and misconceptions come from? What kind of anatomical plumbing would a hippopotamus have in order to burn the burritos at both ends?

The hippopotamus (from the Greek *hippos*, horse, and *potamos*, river) is a semiaquatic, sub-Saharan African animal that comes in two species and sizes: humungous (your run-of-the-mill hippo) and relatively small (the pygmy hippopotamus). Their closest relatives are whales and porpoises, whom their ancestors abandoned some sixty million years ago when they hit the beach. Shaped like huge barrels, hippos spend most of their time in rivers and lakes to buoy their tonnage off their stubby legs, but when they go foraging on dry land in the evenings they can outrun a human—even a Kenyan one-hundred-meter champion. And because they're the third largest land mammal (after elephants and rhinoceroses) and among the grumpiest and most aggressive critters in the animal kingdom, you don't want one of these mad-as-hell megafauna to catch up with you. The expression "getting your ass stomped into the ground" would take on a painfully literal meaning. And to make matters worse, you'd be smelling its breath just before everything went dark.

You also don't want a hippo to fart on you. During a typical evening dinner, they leisurely graze for four to five hours on roughly 150 pounds of grass. That leads to an incredible amount of farting and crapping, which hippos use for marking territory in rivers and lakes by spinning and flicking their tails to distribute it through the water—kind of like the guy who waves his hand around his ass when he farts to make sure everybody gets a good whiff. Except that in the case of hippos, their stink on the water not only makes other male hippos back off but attracts the ladies like Armani Code cologne. Also, when a female hippo wants to mate, she'll dip her face in front of her desired lover and blow flirtatious bubbles through the water—kind of like farting, in other words.

Digestive activity does indeed create both belching and farting, and it's a fairly common old wives' tale, or perhaps just an old wives' joke, that "a burp cheats your ass out of a fart." But oral and anal exhalations come from different parts of the lengthy digestive system. The hippo has only one stomach, but it's divided into three chambers, where microbes take plenty of time breaking down all that cellulose-heavy roughage as it moves along. The third chamber, called the glandular stomach, leads directly to the intestine, where enzymes pick up the job as the stomach's microbes leave off. From the front part of the stomach, all the methane, carbon dioxide, and other gases exit the big lug's mouth—and probably any human close enough to smell it might indeed declare that hippopotami suffer from fart breath. But by definition, it's a belch, not a fart, just as vomit is not diarrhea. The gas created in the long, winding intestine moves toward the rear, and there is only one exit back there, just below that flicking tail that swishes it around like aerosol perfume when it comes out. If the wind ain't exiting that orifice, it ain't a fart. From all reports, if you're standing behind a hippo when it lets one go, you will not confuse it with a burp.

If you're asking why anyone would be even remotely interested in the bubbly breezes emanating from either end of an obese, hairless, and thoroughly antisocial creature, consider that the hippopotamus is one of nature's funniest-looking, pug-ugly creations. Because they spend most of their time submerged underwater, all we normally see of them are two sleepy eyes and huge nostrils and a maw of a mouth with enormous stalagmite teeth. You have to admit, they look pretty ridiculous, which is why cartoonists and animators love them. Just think about those rotund ballerina hippos dancing to "Dance of the Hours" from Ponchielli's *La Gioconda* in the 1940 Walt Disney classic *Fantasia*. Balancing three tons on a pirouette—well, humor doesn't get any better than that. And a flatulent hippo is naturally funnier than, say, a fox with the same problem.

According to the Urban Dictionary, "hippo fart" has become anthropomorphic—"A very large smelly fart, the kind of which you would expect from a two-ton mammal, but actually coming from a human."

On YouTube, gassy hippos have an even bigger audience than gassy elephants, made all the more laughable by the fact that the farts in their watery habitat are usually visible. Champagne should be so effervescent. There's even a video showing a dog that, having ventured close to a hippo, runs away when a big bubble comes up and bursts like a depth charge.

Like the elephant, the hippopotamus has a date with a disastrous destiny. In May 2006 the International Union for Consideration of Nature classified it as a vulnerable species on its Red List, after the Africa-wide population declined as much as 20 percent over the preceding decade, especially in Zimbabwe and the war-torn Democratic Republic of the Congo. An estimated 125,000 to 150,000 hippos are out there right now, blissfully burping from one end and farting from the other, but who knows for how much longer?

28

TWENTY CELEBRITY FARTS

Dateline: Hollywood. Okay, this is really what your inquiring mind wants to know, right? Which film and TV stars fart the most, laugh at farts, tell fart jokes, or pull pranks with whoopee cushions and fart machines on other celebrities? Well, you've come to the right place. I've already outed some of these luminaries—such as Jennifer Aniston, Johnny Depp, Kelsey Grammer, and Whoopi Goldberg—in previous books, but some folks are simply incorrigible, no matter how famous they get. Here are twenty classics to share with your friends:

1. According to Michael Andre D'Estries' June 24, 2008, item in Ecorazzi. com, *Clueless* star Alicia Silverstone, popular in Europe for making a nude French commercial for People for the Ethical Treatment of Animals (PETA), told British TV talk show host Graham Norton, "All four of my dogs are vegan; they don't fart anymore!"

2. At the San Luis Obispo International Film Festival on March 16, 2009, John Waters was asked about the scratch-and-sniff Odorama card, complete with a fart smell (Number 2), that accompanied his popular 1981 film *Polyester.* "I tell you, I went all over the world and people gave me money to smell a fart," he said. "It was an international phenomenon. Rich, poor, Asian, Black, French, any nationality—they'd hear Number 2, they'd hear a fart, and then they'd smell it and give me money."

3. On a junket to promote the 2006 film *Yours, Mine and Ours*, Dennis Quaid complained to Fred Topel of Madblast.com about his kissing scene with a pig. "They smeared stuff on my lips just so the pig would find it appetizing," he said. "It was like out of a garbage can. Not only that, she had gas. After about three takes, you'd have this big pig fart. It was a low, a nadir point in my career." Don't look for Dennis to appear in any *Babe* sequels.

4. On Thursday, September 21, 2006, actress Teri Hatcher brought a plastic cup of Wind Breaker to *Late Night with Jay Leno* and demonstrated it by pushing her fingers into the wet clay to make farting sounds. She called Wind Breaker "a fancy version of Fart Sludge" and said it was popular on the set of ABC's *Desperate Housewives*.

5. Director James Cameron, talking about the bond between Leonardo DiCaprio and Kate Winslet on the set of his 1997 film *Titanic*, told *Rolling Stone* writer David Lipinsky that DiCaprio wore a long coat. "He would, like, fart in it, and then sweep the coat over [Winslet's] face. I mean, if anybody else in the world did that, they'd get slapped, and the other person would walk away and not talk to them for a week."

6. In late July 1999, on the TV quiz show *Celebrity Match Game*, emcee Michael Burger was looking for his four celebrity panelists to finish his sentence when he asked, "Did you hear about the Howard Stern doll? You wind it up and it keeps. . . ." Veteran TV actress Karen Valentine completed the line by writing "Farting." Vicki Lawrence, claiming she never used that word, offered "Bottom burping." Actor-comedian Rondell Sheridan held up "Breaking wind," and actress Nell Carter matched Valentine with "Farting." In discussing the panel's answers, Burger used the word *fart* several times, but don't expect flatulence to become commonplace on these evening game shows until you hear the words "I'll take Farting for $500, Alex."

7. Now we know why Will Ferrell's *Land of the Lost* was a stinker: British costar Anna Friel's fresh vegetable juice diet. "I was the first one to fart," she said on BBC One's *Friday Night with Jonathan Ross* in early 2009. "It

was so awful. I've never been so mortified. I let off the most awful smell. I just felt my face going redder and redder." But nice guy Ferrell blasted a courtesy fart to make her feel better. "Will very kindly built one up," Anna said. "It's possibly the longest, loudest fart I've ever heard. And I thought that's the most gentlemanly thing anyone has ever done for me."

8. Talking with Jeff Gordinier in the Wiseguy column of *Details* magazine, singer Billy Joel said everything went wrong when he was in his early twenties. "I just figured the world didn't need another failed musician. You take yourself so seriously—you've got your head so far up your ass you can't see straight." Looking for poison to drink, he found a bottle of bleach and a bottle of furniture polish in his mother's closet. "And at the time I thought, well, the furniture polish will probably taste better than the bleach, so I'll drink the furniture polish. And all I ended up doing was farting furniture polish for a couple of days and polishing my mother's chairs."

9. Oscar-winning actress Halle Berry told Teenhollywood.com that to prepare for her leading role in *Catwoman*, she adopted an intense exercise regime and drank protein shakes to enhance her muscle-building exercises. But the drinks had an unwanted side effect. "It was wicked stuff," she confessed in the May 31, 2004, item that was subsequently picked up by *Vogue*, the *Sunday Mirror* and many other publications. "I had the worst gas in the world!"

10. Christine Spines, writing about Steven Soderbergh's remaking of the 1960 film *Ocean's Eleven* in *Premiere* magazine, reported, "The farting contest between [Brad] Pitt and [George] Clooney on the Warners jet was one of the production's most patently *South Park* moments. 'When you're at 30,000 feet and you can't crack a window, it can be particularly upsetting,' recalls [screenwriter Ted] Griffin, who was one of the eight passengers aboard. 'Brad came up with the winner, which absolutely flattened all of us.'" The Clooney Network page commented on the midair crepitation, saying that competitive farting "wasn't everyone's idea of a good time but it suited George." Brad Pitt must have picked up his competitive edge

from then-wife Jennifer Aniston, who loves fart jokes. Shortly after their 2000 wedding, Brad declared that matrimony is a gas. "Being married," he explained, "means I can fart and eat ice cream in bed."

11. During a July 20, 2009, interview on MTV, comedy actor Seth Rogen discussed the fart jokes in his newest film, *Funny People*, with Larry Carroll.

> Rogen: I'm trying to remember which jokes actually made it into the movie. [Laughs.] I came up with the farting-on-the-airplane joke. I have to take credit for that.
>
> Carroll: In that joke, you talk about how an airplane is the only place where it's OK to fart, because no one knows who did it. You travel all the time—so, are you guilty of farting on a plane in real life?
>
> Rogen: Oh, definitely. [Laughs.] I just go for it. Farting on a plane is an unrivaled act; it's primal almost.
>
> Carroll: You know, after *Funny People* comes out, no one is going to want to sit near you on a plane.
>
> Rogen: Exactly, yeah. That'll be weird. . . .
>
> Carroll: You've been around funny people your entire life. What is the single greatest joke you've ever heard?
>
> Rogen: If I could fart on cue, I would do that right now—and that would be my answer.

12. One fabled fart hit its mark on the set of the 1983 Oscar-winning film *Terms of Endearment*, during a disagreement between costars Shirley MacLaine and Debra Winger, who were playing mother and daughter. The angry Winger turned her back on MacLaine, lifted her skirt, and broke wind. Many insiders have since alluded to that fart, including the Insider.com, on its list of Difficult Actors: "Debra Winger never met a costar in the early '80s about whom she couldn't find something to hate, from Richard Gere in *An Officer and a Gentleman* to her fart-target screen mom Shirley MacLaine in *Terms of Endearment*."

13. "Penelope Cruz and Johnny Depp had a deep connection on the set [of Ted Demme's 2001 film *Blow*]," says the Internet Movie Database. "They love fart jokes. The pair spent all their time between takes fooling around with whoopee cushions. . . . Cruz admits, 'The more absurd the better. Silly things like this whoopee cushion. I love it! I just want to do it to everybody, but people seem to know it so well.'" In their 2007 Depp biography, Michael Blitz and Louise Krasniewicz wrote, "What audiences did not see was the Johnny Depp offscreen who had purchased a fart machine and was breaking up the cast members with fart sounds at strategic moments in shooting. Costar Penelope Cruz, in particular, found Depp's practical jokes to be hilarious. She said, "Johnny is the funniest man. I don't think people know this but he is always the joker. . . . You know, I am screaming, pulling at my hair [in a scene from *Blow*]. All of a sudden I hear 'pfgggggg' and I think 'Incredible, just ignore it.' But it comes again and I am smiling. Then everybody laughs."

14. According to several sources, the 1968 film set of MGM's *Hello, Dolly!* was a very unhappy place, and nobody clashed more than Walter Matthau and Barbra Streisand. Matthau, age forty, felt his twenty-five-year-old costar was too young for the role of matchmaker Dolly Levi. Furthermore, according to the Turner Movie Classics website, "Matthau is said to have been frustrated with Streisand's demand for retakes and what he saw as an inflated ego. He refused to be in the same room as Streisand unless they were filming and was quoted as saying, 'I have more talent in my smallest fart than she does in her entire body.' The dislike was mutual, with Streisand presenting Matthau with a bar of soap for his 'sewer-mouth.'"

15. Screenwriting team Karen McCullah Lutz and Kirsten Smith, whose credits include *10 Things I Hate About You* (1999) and *Legally Blonde* (2001), told the *New York Times'* John Anderson in 2008: "Miramax is the only studio that's ever told us to add" a fart joke. They were adapting a beloved children's book called *Ella Enchanted* into a 2004 Anne Hathaway film when Harvey Weinstein, Miramax's president, perhaps felt the movie about a medieval princess needed a little more testosterone. The writers injected a gag during

a wedding scene featuring a giant knocking an elf (actor Aidan McArdle) off a bench with a super-size flatus.

16. From what Cameron Diaz told *Esquire*'s Bill Zehme, things got a little childish on the set of the 2000 film *Charlie's Angels*. "I love talking about [farting]," she said. "One of the biggest conversational pleasures I know is to indulge yourself in a little flatulent humor. There are no inhibitions here." She and costars Drew Barrymore and Lucy Liu outdid each other making gross fart noises with their mouths. "We're now known for that," Diaz said proudly, and mentioned that she keeps a fart machine at home for unsuspecting guests. "It's the best," she said. "It's like drugs. The first time you do it to somebody who's not expecting it—man, it's just the greatest high!" She also confessed to Zehme that sometimes when she catches a whiff of a fart, she'll compliment the offender whether she knows him/her or not. Zehme added that Diaz got high praise from Bobby Farrelly, who codirected her breakthrough 1998 movie *There's Something About Mary*. "Cameron's like Grace Kelly—but with gas," Farrelly said.

17. For a regular dose of TV flatulence, you should check out CBS's *Late Late Night with Craig Ferguson*. If the Scottish-born host isn't talking about his gassy dogs, he's sniggering about cracks in general. For example, on February 17, 2009, political comedian Bill Maher sat with Ferguson bemoaning the loss of George W. Bush as a source of jokes. "Bush was so easy," Maher groused, then asked Ferguson, "Are you having trouble doing jokes about Obama?" Ferguson leaned forward with one of his Cheshire cat grins. "I do fart jokes, Bill."

Ferguson favors the adjective *farty*—not generally used in America, but he's probably changing that. On March 3, 2009, he asked Paris Hilton, "Are your dogs farty? Five dogs, no farts?" and confessed that his own French bulldog is "very farty." When CNN's Larry King showed up on June 11, 2009, Ferguson told him that he'd heard a rumor that "you were farty." Ferguson had already set up the comment ahead of time by telling the audience during his monologue that "[Larry] is a farty King," as he swept his hand toward the empty guest chair, and added that he might be doing more of *this* (moving his hand back and forth in a sweeping fashion) after Larry King came on and sat down.

18. Rolling Stones guitarist Keith Richards is a big fan of Buddy Holly, the Texas rocker best known today for his brilliant career decision to perish in an iconic 1959 plane crash. The Rolling Stones' first American hit was a remake of Holly's "Not Fade Away." In his 2009 memoir *Under Their Thumb*, Bill German, who created the Stones' *Beggars Banquet* fanzine, recalled an impromptu jam between Richards and Stones rhythm guitarist Ron Wood in Wood's kitchen. Playing acoustic guitars, "they began fooling around with Buddy Holly covers," including "Peggy Sue" and "Rave On," with Keith doing most of the singing. But soon "their jam that night devolved into an earth-shattering fart contest," said German. "Some serious Hall of Fame cheese-cutting. In the middle of 'Not Fade Away' [perhaps at the line "I try to show you but you drive me back"] Keith stopped, lifted his guitar, and went POOF! Woody answered with one of his own. They alternated flatulence for three or four more songs. 'That'll be the day-ay-ay that I—' *Zap!* I told Keith, 'You're a real farter figure to me.'"

19. Today's hyper-choreographed pop stars often get winded during their onstage routines, but California diva Katy Perry seems to merely get wind. Talking with Florence Welch for MySpace, Katy, famous for her smash single "I Kissed a Girl," confessed in early 2009 that her vigorous dancing often adds a little extra crackle to her show's excitement. "I fart a lot. I'm hopping around. I'm a little gassy. I don't care. It's my stage." No wonder her hit 2008 album on Capitol Records was called *One of the Boys*.

20. Megan Fox, slinky star of both Hollywood and the Internet, got sci-fi and fantasy fanboys excited after she spoke with *GQ* writer Mark Kirby at the crowded 2008 Comic-Con(vention) in San Diego, where her role in *Transformers* the previous year qualified her as a genuine sex goddess whose butt bubbles would have smelled of roses and rainbows. When the subject turned to farts, the sassy siren was quite an expert: "If you eat Chinese food, your farts come out like Chinese food," she said. "If you eat

Mexican food, your farts come out like Mexican food. And milk, it's like—you can smell the warmth in the fart. My wardrobe on *Transformers* always smells like farts, and I have no idea why." After talking with a few fans and buying some comic books from vendors, Megan slipped away, whispering to Kirby as they left, "That place smelled like milk farts."

29

LET THE WIND BLOW FREE!

In early 2008 England's *Daily Telegraph* enlisted the public's help in a search for the country's "most remarkable epitaph." The venerable graveside inscription (*epitaph* is literally the ancient Greek word for "on the tombstone") was fast becoming extinct, as weathering, destruction, and vandalism were taking a terrible toll on the country's windswept churchyards. Every year, "25,000 gravestones are lost and with them the important historical information they contain," said the *Telegraph*.

That's why Richard Stuart, director of the National Archive of Memorial Inscriptions, was on a desperate mission to record as many epitaphs as possible while they were still legible—or still around. In partnership with *BBC History Magazine*, Stuart launched a Mysterious Memorials competition to coax readers into submitting the most interesting or bizarre epitaphs they'd ever seen. "These inscriptions contain unique information not found anywhere else before the 1840s," Stuart told writer Caroline Davies. "Some people put a lot of effort into thinking exactly what they want on their tombstone. It's their last words on earth, and they want them to be just right." Before England's first census in 1841 and the first Births, Deaths, and Marriages register four years earlier, these epitaphs, dates, and familial markings (such as "beloved son of") were often the only sources of genealogical information that people left behind.

In the blizzard of reader entries, one epitaph kept turning up in various wordings. It seemed to be a warning to the visitor that holding back his farts might hasten his own final repose.

A typical submission was "Let the wind go free/ Wherever thou may be/ Because it was the wind that killed me."

A Dr. Edward Black wrote that he'd seen "Where e'er ye be let your wind fly free for wind hath been the death of me" at the Norfolk Coast Churchyard south of Cromer. An anonymous reader reported that he saw a gravestone in St. Saviours, Aston, Birmingham, that read: "Wherever ye be, let your wind blow free, for the want of a fart was the death of me." Reader John LeFebvre claimed he couldn't attest firsthand to the veracity of his entry: "My Grandfather always told me of this epitaph, purportedly of a rather flatulent man, 'Where'er you be Let the wind go free For holding it Was the death of me.'" Another reader referred to a "famous tombstone" with the inscription "Wherever you be, let the wind blow free, for holding it in was the death of me." The slight variations were endless.

Surprisingly, nobody pointed out that British novelist William Golding, whose best-known work is *Lord of the Flies*, wrote in *Rites of Passage* (1980) that "As the epitaph says, whatever you be let your wind go free for holding mine was the death of me."

Was this a joke? Could the lack of a good fart really kill you, or at least ruin your health and lead to an early grave? Certainly the Greek physician Hippocrates thought so, and who am I to argue with the man for whom modern medicine's Hippocratic oath is named? "It is best for flatulence to pass without noise a-breaking," he wrote in 420 B.C.E., "though it is better for it to pass with noise than to be intercepted and accumulated internally." The Romans were big defenders of unfettered farting. In 41 A.D., Emperor Claudius, according to his biographer Suetonius Tranquillus, "planned an edict to legitimize the breaking of wind at table, either silently or noisily, after hearing about a man who was so modest that he endangered his health by an attempt to restrain himself." Roughly 150 years later, writer Gaius Petronius made a similar diagnosis in *Satyricon*: "Take my word for it, friends, the vapors go straight to your brain. Poison your whole system. I know some who've died from being too polite and holding it in." Much later, the sixteenth-century French essayist Michel de Montaigne lamented in "Of the Power of the Imagination" that "the refusing of one single fart, may bring us to the very gates of a most excruciating death." Even Sir Thomas More, in a 1518 epigram called "On Breaking Wind," wrote, "Wind, if you keep it too long in your stomach, kills you; on the other hand, it can save your life if it is properly let out."

The line "let the wind blow free" had been breezing around for quite a while in a nonfarting context. It goes back at least to a 1760s sea shanty called "The Keeper of the Eddystone Light," a tale about a lighthouse near Portsmouth, England, that later turned up as a folk song ("Eddystone Light") on a 1993 Peter, Paul & Mary album:

> Yo-ho-ho, the wind blows free,
> It's all for the life on the rolling sea!

In sea shanties—the chantlike songs that sailors used to maintain synchronicity while they worked—letting the wind blow free was a declaration of an adventurer's open-ended life, unburdened by domestic responsibilities. He let the trade winds carry him where they were wont to go.

"Let the wind go free" has been a common variant, for as the wind goes, it can *go* free or *blow* free—they're almost one and the same. One simply lets nature take its course. The only difference, in human terms, is that *go* suggests passive release, while *blow* requires perhaps a little grunt and a squeeze to shove it into the world.

In 1922 James Joyce put the gentler term into Molly Bloom's internal monologue in the "Penelope" section of *Ulysses*: "that was a relief wherever you be let your wind go free." In his 1999 memoirs, *A British Tale of Indian and Foreign Service*, Sir Ian Scott recalled a dark Anglo-Indian nanny he engaged for his daughter in Peshawar in 1939. "She proved expert enough with the baby, applying generally her various aphorisms, such as 'Where you be, let the wind go free.'" British writer Melvyn Bragg, in his 1999 novel *The Soldier's Return*, wrote, "He eased himself in his seat to let the wind go free."

These days, cemeteries have been replaced by vast memorial gardens, which typically limit stones to small, ground-level markers with nothing more than a name and two book-end years. But what about the epitaph?

There's a well-known piece of anonymous doggerel called "Tae a Fart," written in the style of the late eighteenth-century poet Robert Burns and based loosely on his "To a Mouse," that recounts the "horrible beastie [that] lurks in yer stomach efter a feastie." Before long "[t]here starts to stir a michty wind," as the vittles get to work. Finally,

> Michty me! A sonic boom! . . .
> Where e'er ye be, Let yer wind gang free.

Now try putting *that* on your flat little gravestone.

30

THE LOW-FART MARSUPIAL DIET

It's big, dumb, and silly looking, and it's one of Australia's biggest pests, bouncing around on rooftops, crashing into cars, and sometimes smashing through plate-glass windows. But Aussies also consider the kangaroo one of their national treasures, lovable in its own doofus way and blessed with its own place of honor on the national crest. In May 2009, when the state of Canberra licensed marksmen to cull its mushrooming "roo" population, the rest of the country raised an outcry that brought the program to a halt more screeching than a kangaroo slamming into the side of a freight train.

And now, lo and behold, love 'em or hate 'em, it looks like roos may offer their own special salvation to Australia's—and perhaps the world's—pollution problem. Why? Because their farts are earth-friendly. Thanks to special bacteria in their stomachs, kangaroos don't produce methane, the greenhouse gas so abundant in the flatulence of other mammals. And in the lab, scientists say they are just a hop, skip, and a jump away from isolating those bacteria and transplanting them into other grazing animals—three years, tops . . . well, maybe four or five. Six if they're lucky.

"Fourteen percent of emissions from all sources in Australia is from enteric methane from cattle and sheep," Queensland scientist Athol Klieve told Agence France Presse in 2007. "And if you look at another country such as New Zealand, which has got a much higher agricultural base, they're actually up around 50 percent." Gastrointestinal bacteria from kangaroos would make those animals' digestion much more efficient and save farmers millions of dollars in feed costs. "Not only would [livestock] not produce the methane, they would actually get something like 10 to 15 percent more energy out of the feed they are eating," Klieve said. All these gains, of course, would be moot if such an introduction of foreign digestive bacteria into ruminant animals' stomachs had the same kind of unintended consequences as Australia's disastrous importation of rabbits in the nineteenth century.

The news prompted many health-conscious Australians to wonder if maybe farmers should just get out of the barnyard business altogether and start raising free-ranging, low-emission kangaroos for food. Reportedly up to 20 percent of the continent's human population already eats roo meat because it's low-fat and high-protein, so why not encourage the other 80 percent? It would solve both the kangaroo overpopulation problem and the damage that nonnative cattle and sheep inflict on Australia's semi-arid grasslands. The lack of methane farts would simply be the icing on the cake.

In a detailed 2008 study published in *Conservation Letters*, Dr. George R. Wilson of Australian Wildlife Services in Canberra, along with Melanie J. Edwards, explained that kangaroos produce negligble amounts of methane because they are "nonruminant forestomach fermenters" as opposed to ruminant livestock with several stomachs. If farmers removed "seven million cattle and thirty-six million sheep by 2020" and replaced them by increasing the number of native kangaroos to 175 million, they could produce the same amount of meat and "lower Australia's [greenhouse gas] emissions by 16 megatonnes, or 3% of Australia's annual emissions." The switch would also save farmers from paying any future "permit fees," or "fart taxes," on their animals if the government gets around to instituting its proposed "Emissions Trading Scheme" in 2010 as a way to cap and trade greenhouse gases. But it would require "large cultural and social adjustments and reinvestment."

Ben Harder, reporting for *U.S. News & World Report*, saw how kanga-roos might even help the human population. "I've read that the flatulence of 1 in every 3 adults contains [excessive] methane, and parents sometimes pass the trait to their children. Will families of methane-makers soon be encouraged to swallow little capsules of kangaroo microbes?"

Hey, I'm all for it, as long as switching to kangaroo stomach flora is strictly voluntary. On the other hand, if a government edict tried to force me into a methane-free diet, I'd be hopping mad.

31

SIGHING ORIFICES: THE TWAIN SHALL MEET

American humorist Samuel L. Clemens, or Mark Twain as he's better remembered, knew a thing or two about farting. He's famous, at least among academics, for a satirical commentary—one of his "fugitive pieces," he called it—in which he likened masturbation to farting. Yes, jackin' off and crackin' off, circle jerks and farting contests—two sides of the same coin, at least when guys got together. With the demeanor of a typical moral reformer of the day, Twain delivered the speech in spring 1879 to the Stomach Club, a dining and drinking fraternity of artistic American expats living in Paris. The title was "Some Thoughts on the Science of Onanism."

Onan, in case you've forgotten, was the classic *schlimazel*, a no-luck guy who appeared in the Book of Genesis, Chapter 38, just long enough to get knocked off. Onan's father, Judah, had asked him to impregnate his older brother Er's widow, Tamar, in order that Er would have an heir. But during intercourse Onan defied his father (and God) by pulling out at the last second and "spilling his seed on the ground," because he didn't want to make any babies he couldn't claim for his own lineage. God was so pissed off that he killed him. (God was more of a hothead in those days, before he had a kid of his own.) Onan's crime wasn't masturbation, or even *coitus interruptus* for that matter, but rather disobedience—because defying or disrespecting one's parents was a capital offense under the Holiness Codes outlined in Leviticus. But Jews and Christians needed a biblical example to scare their boys away from spanking the monkey, so Onan, having dumped his semen uselessly outside Tamar's womb, became the pud-pounding patsy and all-around wicked wanker.

Noting that the speaker before him had already exhausted the "social evil" of adultery, Mark Twain told the jolly, after-dinner crowd, "I will continue his good work in the cause of morality by cautioning you against that species of recreation called self-abuse to which I perceive you are much addicted." He "quoted" many personages who had spoken favorably of masturbation, including Queen Elizabeth ("It is the bulwark of virginity"), the Zulu leader Cetewayo ("A jerk in the hand is worth two in the bush") and Benjamin Franklin ("Masturbation is the best policy").

Finally, in the penultimate paragraph, he got to the meat of the matter: "Of all the kinds of sexual intercourse, this has least to recommend it. As an amusement it is too fleeting, as an occupation it is too wearing, as a public exhibition there is no money in it. It has, in our last day of progress and improvement, been degraded to brotherhood with flatulence—among the best bred these two arts are now indulged only in private—though by consent of the whole company, when only males are present, it is still permissible, in good society, to remove the embargo upon the fundamental sigh."

Twain appears to be defining this "fundamental sigh" as both a vocal release of air during the primal act of ejaculation, *and* an airy anal release that's available to us much more frequently and without making a mess (well, mostly). After all, one definition of sigh is "a sound made by the wind," as when Sir Walter Scott wrote in his 1810 poem, "Lady of the Lake," "Creeping shrubs, of thousand dyes, Waved in the west-wind's summer sighs."

Next time you hear a butt rumble or smell a stench of barnyard proportions, don't ask, "Who farted?" Politely inquire, "Fundamentally, whom may I ask is responsible for that sigh?"

32

REALITY BITES BUBBLES IN A BATHTUB!

The British press simply called her Sophie, and the British public needed nothing further. Sophie—Sophie Reade, if you're asking—was the boobacious (only recently enhanced), glamour-puss blonde on Channel 4's reality show *Big Brother 10*, burning up the tabloid press. For example, the *Mirror*, on September 4, 2009, announced "Sophie Insistent She Won't Get Back with Kris," after she informed her housemates—the remaining people with whom she had shared the tenth season isolated in a custom-built house—that her relationship with the churlish, curly, burly brute was over because he hadn't denied the rumors that they were having sex early in the season. Besides, viewers had already voted Kris off the show in July, and Sophie was not only still there but favored by the oddsmakers to win that very evening.

The hottest news of the day, besides the breakup of Sophie and Kris, was that thanks to Sophie's annoying habit of boldly farting at everybody, one of Great Britain's top pharmaceutical companies had made her "a tempting offer . . . to advertise their anti-flatulence capsules when she leaves the house." The only question now was, with *Big Brother 10* scheduled to end its summer run within a few hours, how big would Sophie win?

Sophie was a natural drama queen, a walking, talking train wreck of a girl who had managed to get everyone's attention early in the show when she and Kris began what seemed like a steamy, stormy affair. Romances had become suspect on *Big Brother* because participants in the earlier seasons had learned that TV viewers—the ones with the power to vote housemates off the show with just a click or a phone call—were reluctant to break up ongoing relationships, especially the ones filled with the kind of *sturm und drang* that etched itself vividly into the public imagination. As Jody Thompson reported in *The Mirror* on June 29, "Big Brother has, unsurprisingly, grilled Kris about his supposed relationship with Sophie, after housemates were told in no uncertain terms that 'fake romances will not be tolerated' this year." But Kris "insisted that their relationship is for real—well, about as real as a tryst can be between two people utterly obsessed with themselves"—because "they farted in front of each other." Kris explained that getting intimate enough to start farting "usually takes around three months but in here it's been three weeks. . . . Sophie trumps all the time." Who could question the sincerity of a love like that?

Near the end of July, on day fifty-five, after Kris had left the show, Sophie set the nation atwitter when she shared a morning bath with cute lad (and ultimate final-five finalist) Rodrigo and splashed him with a couple of big fart bubbles. The program's chat rooms and blog threads buzzed for days. As reported by Digital Spy's Matthew Reynolds:

"Oooh Sophie, stop. Stop farting. It's disgusting," Rodrigo said, moving down to the other end of the bath.

"I can't help it," she replied, blaming her lentil diet.

"Did you eat cabbage last night? It's disrespectful," he said.

Siavash [another housemate, an Iranian-born fashionista wannabe] interrupted to wind Rodrigo up, saying: "You were farting in your sleep last night, Rodrigo."

"I was not," he replied.

"You were," said Siavash.

"A loud one," added Sophie.

She then admitted to her problem. "I don't know what's wrong with me. I've got really, really bad wind," she said.

This was dramatic television at its best. Eat your heart out, Paddy Chayefsky. Even more noteworthy, it was the biggest event to occur in a bathtub since the Greek mathematician Archimedes realized 2,200 years ago that he could figure out how much he weighed by measuring how much water he displaced. Unfortunately, Sophie and Rodrigo denied themselves Archimedes' "Eureka!" moment by not consulting the slide-rule app on their smartphones and calculating the volume of her fart bubbles.

By day eighty-five—August 26—Sophie was bemoaning the fact "that no-one will take her seriously after her appearance on *Big Brother*," according to another Digital Spy reporter, Catriona Wightman. "Sitting in the living area, Marcus joked that she had 'ruined it' by swearing, farting and stealing.

"'I fart, I burp,' Sophie agreed. 'Guys aren't going to think I'm very ladylike.'"

When the final eviction hour drew nigh, as *Big Brother 10*'s two million–plus regular viewers and who knows how many tabloid addicts breathlessly looked on, after ninety-three days and the dwindling of twenty-two housemates into a final five, veteran MTV hostess Davina McCall, her dark hair coiffed like a demented rockabilly princess, stood outside the house delivering her catchphrase—"Big Brother House, this is Davina. You are live on Channel 4, please do not swear"—and then began evicting the three runners-up one by one with yet another trademark line: "You have thirty seconds to say your goodbyes; I'm coming to get you!"

And finally, after the three had been called out of the house and interviewed, it was down to Sophie and Siavash, and Davina was ready to announce the name of the lucky winner who, according to Heidi Stephens of *The Guardian*, would "walk the walkway to either a C-list celebrity lifestyle in the style of Brian Dowling, or total obscurity, à la last year's winner, Rachel Rice. Remember her? Nope, me neither." Heidi was personally betting on "glamour girl-next-door Sophie, who, after the departure of controlling twit Kris, proved herself to be sweet, funny, charming, and thoroughly up for a laugh. If she manages to ditch both the godawful hair extensions and Kris, she'll be thoroughly worthy of the inevitable spread in *Nuts* magazine [a topless girlie weekly]."

Cut to Davina in her silver sequined jacket, rooster updo still towering: "The winner is . . . Sophie!"

Sophie was stunned. "I've not won," she exclaimed to Siavash, who had finished a distant second place. The two were grabbing and hugging each other in—shock? Siavash gushed, "You've done it," as if Sophie had just been awarded a Nobel prize for curing AIDS *and* hemorrhoids in one fell swoop. Siavash looked almost happy that it was the twenty-year-old farting floozie, and not him, walking off with £71,000 in prize money (that's over $100,000).

Heidi Stephens, her claws clicking over the computer keys, picked up the play-by-play: "10.36 p.m.: In the house, Sophie is still looking shell-shocked. She also appears to be hitting the wine, and anyone who has ever seen Sophie pissed [drunk] will know that doesn't bode well at ALL. . . . 10.48 p.m.: Reasons why we love Sophie—she burps, falls over when drunk, eats cake, and looks a total mess without makeup. . . . A worthy winner, in my book—well done, Sophie."

Now the big question was: will Sophie be the spokeswoman for a fart remedy? As the *Sun*'s Dan Menhinnitt explained it, "The glamour model has upset other housemates by openly farting in the house, and wound up Rodrigo Lopes by doing it while the pair shared a bath. But her digestion problems could prove to be a money maker as she's going to be asked to front a six-figure national publicity campaign for WindSetlers once she's out of the Big Brother house." Or as a prescient fan put it, blogging at ThisIsBigBrother.com on the night of Sophie's victory, "Wow, looks like she's going to go far(t) after the show!"

And go far she did. WindSetlers—gel capsules containing activated dimeticone that breaks down bubbles in the stomach, whose tag line is "Blow Away Trapped Wind!"—come not from a mom-and-pop herbal operation but rather Thornton & Ross, a venerable Yorkshire-based manufacturer of household disinfectants, hygiene products, and pharmaceuticals. Sophie would be a corporate spokesfarter. As a WindSetlers representative told Menhinnitt: "Bloating and trapped wind cause discomfort and embarrassment for thousands of women [nearly 40 percent, according to a recent WindSetlers survey] across the country, yet it is still considered a taboo subject and is not often discussed. We hope the fact that young Sophie has been so vocal and carefree about her excessive wind will encourage women specifically to talk more openly about a condition that affects us all to some degree and not be so embarrassed about seeking out treatment."

So Sophie goes from Big Brother winner to Big Sister of every guilt-ridden gassy girl in England's green—and beyond. It's a victory for everyone. Except poor Kris, of course.

33

HOLLYWOOD'S NO-FARTING ZONE

You knew it had to happen sooner or later. After thirty-five years of Tin-seltown toots and tuchus tantrums, from blasting buckaroo buttholes in *Blazing Saddles* (1974) to Seth Rogen's fuming fart flume in *Funny People* (2009), film critics have settled on a shopworn phrase to sum up a movie's family friendliness: "No fart jokes!" or put more delicately, no flatulence jokes.

The trend may have started in 1998, when a special movie rating web-page for concerned parents (parentpreviews.com) praised Disney's *The Jungle Book: Mowgli's Story* because "it's aimed at a young audience and has no flatulence jokes, crotch-kicking scenes, or unnecessary violence."

Regular media critics picked up the line the following year, in 1999, when the *Pittsburgh Post-Gazette*'s Tony Norman ended his review of the Japanese animated import *Princess Mononoke* with: "Sorry, no flatulence jokes or postmodern navel gazing here—just good old-fashioned storytell-ing by master director Hayao Miyazaki."

"Stiller/Wilson fans anticipating another *Meet the Parents* or *Zoolander* will find themselves adrift in unexpectedly offbeat and cerebral territory," critic James Berardinelli at ReelViews wrote two years later about *The Royal Tenenbaums*. "There are no flatulence jokes and little in the way of physical humor."

In 2001, Heather Wadowski noted in a review for Suite101.com: "*The Princess Diaries* features no gross-out humor, no fart jokes—nothing offensive at all."

Chris Gore at *Film Threat* magazine, trashing George Lucas's *Star Wars: Episode 1—The Phantom Menace* in May 2002, complained, "Three fart jokes. Count them—three. I remember reading somewhere that Lucas wanted this film to be an epic on the scale of *Lawrence of Arabia*, which, strangely enough, features no fart jokes at all."

Rotten Tomatoes critic Eric D. Snider said of Martin Lawrence's 2005 bomb *Rebound*, "The movie's bad, but at least it isn't aggressively annoying. It has puke jokes, but hey—no farts! Put *those* quotes in your ads, 20th Century Fox."

The antifart hysteria was hitting a crescendo in early September 2008 when an unimpressed *Chicago Tribune* reader, responding to the news that Harold Ramis was going to direct *Ghostbusters III*, sent the editor a likely script:

> Seth Rogen sees a ghost.
> Jonah Hill goes "Holy ****ing ****, dude!!"
> Seth Rogen farts.
> They both laugh.
> (Repeat for two hours.)

TheMovieBoy.com's Dustin Putman, in his October 24, 2008, review of the R-rated *Zack and Miri Make a Porno*, wrote, "[T]he film's comedy relies on raunchiness of the sex and bodily function variety (there are no farts, but there is much, much worse), as well as just plain outrageous ideas."

Robert Knaus, discussing Dreamworks' animated *Kung Fu Panda* (2008) for DVDinMyPants.com, said, "First off, it's remarkable what the film doesn't contain. There's . . . not one bodily-function reference (no burps, no farts, no shit)."

After Edward McNulty of the Presbyterian News Service (pcusa.org) served on the Montreal World Film Festival's jury, he weakly praised French director Ricardo Troggi's *1981* in this August 2009 entry: "Although it contains some profanity (which somehow seems muted by subtitles), there are no fart jokes and other such vulgarism that obsess so many American filmmakers when focusing upon childhood or adolescence."

The way these people talk, you'd think movie fart jokes are a bad thing. Oh, it's okay if Hollywood shows pedophilia, necrophilia, and grab-a-feelia, but please—just don't gag us with fart gags.

You have to consider, of course, that this "no fart jokes" commendation is a reaction to Hollywood overkill. As Mike Thomas pointed out in a 2007 *Chicago Sun-Times* article called "Where the Wind Blows," Mel Brooks' cowboy campfire scene in *Blazing Saddles* opened the gas flume, and "from then on films and farts enjoyed a more fruitful collaboration." (For a more detailed history, check out "Gone with the Wind" in *Who Cut the Cheese?*) Several male stars—Mike Myers, Jim Carrey, Will Ferrell, and Seth Rogen among them—have practically built their careers on gross-out scenes of combustible comedy. Television, especially cable, has abetted the trend, particularly with animated material like Comedy Central's *South Park*, which even had its own *The Terrance and Phillip Show* starring a couple of mindless Canadians who did nothing but pass gas at each other to pass the time.

Perhaps it's time for the Motion Picture Association of America to add a new category to its rating system: R, PG-13, PG, G, NFJ (No Fart Jokes).

34

DID A MOOSE LET LOOSE?

So far we've discussed the flatulence of dogs, cows, hippos, kangaroos, and elephants, so what's left? Why, the moose, of course: that big, shy, gawky winter wanderer—perhaps the least charismatic of the deer family—with a huge rack of antlers and an outsized jaw that makes even Jay Leno point and laugh.

The moose is the animal kingdom's Rodney Dangerfield. It gets zero respect. Like its deer, elk, and caribou cousins, its name is both singular and plural no matter how many of them are coming at you; there's no such thing as meese (which is a blessing, I guess, because meese sounds even sillier than moose). It's an Algonquian word meaning "twig eater"—a *twig* eater, for Pete's sake, suggesting that *Prelude to the Afternoon of a Faun* should be the soundtrack as the moose daintily nibbles in the forest. Probably the most famous moose in American culture is an obtuse cartoon character named Bullwinkle whose punch-drunk voice is in the key of "Duh!" (In real life, the moose call is a raspy, basso groan that hunters duplicate by blowing through a funnel or a small hollow log.) During her unsuccessful 2008 vice-presidential campaign, Alaska governor Sarah Palin tried to establish her tough-guy cred by bragging about how she had shot and field dressed a seven-foot moose—even though by firing a high-powered rifle from a helicopter she hadn't exactly given the poor guy a fighting chance. My guess is that in a fair fight, a moose would seriously kick Sarah Palin's ass all the way back to Wasilla—and maybe even as far as Moose Jaw, Saskatchewan.

But here's the worst part. Even in Norway, where this ruminant oaf is the national mascot, the moose has no juice and gets lots of abuse. In August 2007, scientists at the Norwegian Institute of Science and Technology in Torsend blamed the local rise in global warming on the average Scandinavian moose, which—thanks to its four-chambered stomach laboring to digest its leafy, twiggy diet—burps and farts an estimated 2,100 kilos (4,620 pounds) of carbon dioxide a year, equal to what an average Norwegian car would exhaust during a 13,000-kilometer (8,060-mile) trip. Considering that roughly 120,000 moose were roaming Norway's gloaming and fording the fjords, their environmental devastation was the same as if Norwegian motorists were driving an extra 969,340,195 miles, enough to get them to the moon and back over four thousand times, provided their little European cars' antigravity feature was working properly. Even as far away as America, Fox News, on August 22, 2007, trumpeted "Moose Gas Hurting Environment!"—probably to divert Fox viewers' attention from the environmental crimes of American corporations. Talk about the perfect fall guy. We humans drive hundreds of millions of pollution-hacking vehicles and pump billions of tons of industrial crud into the air, yet the fart-happy moose is the one setting us up for the Apocalypse.

It gets worse. Spiegel Online International suggested that the moose problem might not turn out so bad after all, because Norway's hunting season was coming up in late September and hunters were expected to cull the windy culprits by bagging around thirty-five thousand of them. Moose meat happens to be low-fat and tastes like veal or beef.

You can hear a moose fart at moosefart.org. While you're online you can also order "A Small Jug of Moose Farts with a Cork on Top"—a gag gift from Bonanzle.com.

But those of us who mourn the future of this noble animal, along with the fate of our planet, can simply go to the nearest cocktail bar and order a

Moose Fart. It's one part vodka, one part whiskey, one part coffee liqueur, and one part Bailey's Irish Cream—blended with ice to a rich consistency. Webtender.com suggests that since the drink tastes so good, it's best to be generous with the booze and mix a pitcher's worth.

You'll need that pitcher's worth if, like me, you plan to spend a few hours toasting the gassy, twig-munching moose: mankind's patsy and nature's hapless victim.

35

STEP AWAY FROM THE FART MACHINE!

Almost thirty years ago, James Q. Wilson and George L. Kelling wrote an article called "Broken Windows" for the March 1982 edition of the *Atlantic Monthly*. Their thesis was that if police want to reduce serious crime in an area, they have to fix smaller problems first. Their title summed up their Exhibit A: "a building with a few broken windows. If the windows are not repaired, the tendency is for vandals to break a few more windows. Eventually, they may even break into the building, and if it's unoccupied, perhaps become squatters or light fires inside." Crime, in other words, is incremental, and today's untended-to nuisance becomes tomorrow's New Jack City.

Well, how about "the broken wind" theory? If you stop people from letting off one-cheek sneaks and silent-but-deadly farts now, you'll interrupt their butt-slide down that slippery slope to where they'll be asking strangers to "Pull my finger" or bending over and farting on the heads of little children.

Take, for example, the following hard case: on April 8, 2009, the Associated Press reported that "Five men from the Houston area were sharing a Waco [Texas] motel room last night, and two were inside the room eating—when one had a flatulence problem." Okay, so far, so good. Everybody farts—no harm, no foul. But wait. "Police say one man was so upset that he threw a large knife at the odor offender—cutting his leg, and then stabbed him in the chest."

The *Lariat*, a student paper at nearby Baylor University, gave a bit more detail. Juan Antonio Salano Castellano, age thirty-five, was alone in a room at the Clarion Inn with thirty-three-year-old Jose Braule Ramirez. Suddenly "Castellano passed gas. The flatulent act enraged [Ramirez], who threw a large kitchen knife across the room.... The hurled knife cut Castellano on his leg. The man then walked across the hotel room, picked up the kitchen knife and stabbed Castellano in the left side of his chest, the Waco police said."

The victim was taken to the Hillcrest Baptist Medical Center and treated for what appeared to be non-life-threatening injuries, while police ran his erstwhile friend down to the McLennan County Jail and charged him with aggravated assault with a deadly weapon and, the next day, put him on an immigration hold, meaning he couldn't be released on the $15,000 bond set for him until police verified his status. He was facing between two and twenty years in prison and a fine of up to $10,000.

It's an easy road to perdition, my friends. Today you're farting into a jug, tomorrow *you're* in the jug. Where will it all lead?

The broken wind theory also applies to criminals on the lam. Take, for example, the case of a twenty-nine-year-old resident of Hadersley in Denmark, as reported in a 2009 item in the *Copenhagen Post*. Out on bail, the man was supposed to begin serving multiple sentences in early December of 2008, but he decided not to turn himself in. Three months later, on March 25, a tip led local police to an address on Kløvervej Road. At first they couldn't find him, until "a horrible smell led them to a closet, where they found the man hiding under a pile of clothes." No police dog was needed—that's how bad this guy stunk up the place. Something was indeed rotten in the state of Denmark. Jens Peter Rudbeck, chief inspector with Southern Jutland Police, said, "It was probably the excitement that caused him to pass wind and it was the smell that led us to [him]."

All right, so the guy's been arrested and hauled into court, but even there a guy with too much gas can get into trouble if he's on that slippery slope. Take the case of Joe Francis, the producer of the *Girls Gone Wild* videos that feature college girls flashing their boobs at Mardi Gras in New Orleans, spring break in Daytona Beach, and wet T-shirt contests everywhere. According to a 2009 story in the *Las Vegas Sun*, "Joe Francis went wild in a court deposition this year, and he's being handed a hefty bill as a result." While being questioned earlier that year in Baker, California, by lawyers from the Wynn Las Vegas Casino, Francis not only "improperly asserted his Fifth Amendment right against self-incrimination in refusing to answer even the most innocuous questions," but "openly passed gas, further disrespecting the legal proceeding," said the Wynn attorneys. "As the court will see from reviewing the video clips of Francis' deposition, his utter contempt for the judicial system is apparent, including his repeated attempts to disrupt the deposition with flatulence." The deposition took place in California because Francis was already facing federal tax evasion charges in Los Angeles and couldn't leave the state. District Judge Michelle Leavitt ordered Francis to pay Wynn Las Vegas his $2 million gambling debt, plus interest and court costs that could eventually total $3 million.

Okay, so now the miscreant is in custody. Let's go to South Charleston, West Virginia, where a man who farted was charged with battery on a police officer. According to the *Los Angeles Times*, the Associated Press reported: "Jose A. Cruz, 34, of Clarksburg, was pulled over early Tuesday for driving without headlights, police said. According to the criminal complaint, Cruz smelled of alcohol, had slurred speech and failed three field sobriety tests before he was handcuffed and taken to a police station for a breathalyzer test. As Patrolman T. E. Parsons prepared the machine, Cruz scooted his chair toward Parsons, lifted his leg and 'passed gas loudly.'"

If that weren't bad enough, Cruz "fanned the gas toward the officer." The complaint alleged, "The gas was very odorous and created contact of an insulting or provoking nature with Patrolman Parsons." Cruz admitted letting a few farts, but he denied moving his chair toward the officer or aiming them at him. He said he had an upset stomach, and the police wouldn't let him go to the bathroom. "I couldn't hold it no more," he said, adding that the officers had all laughed along with him while he was farting. "This is ridiculous," Cruz moaned. "I could be facing time."

All right, so now our Jack the Ripper is confined in a small cell where, unless he's in solitary confinement, breaking wind can really get him into trouble. Take the case of Brian Bruggeman from Hershey, Nebraska, as reported by Yahoo! News on December 27, 2006. Two weeks earlier he was in the Lincoln County Jail, serving a ninety-day sentence for violating a protection order, when his farting intruded on his cellmate, robbery suspect Jesse Dorris, and sparked a fight between them that led to Dorris's injury. "Now Bruggeman, 38, faces a Jan. 11 preliminary hearing on the state's complaint of assault by a confined person," reported the article. "It's a felony punishable by up to five years in prison."

According to the *North Platte Bulletin*, here's how the crime went down: "Guards were first alerted to the problem Dec. 14 when inmate Jesse Dorris began banging on his cell door, screaming he wanted out of his cell. . . . Dorris couldn't stand Bruggeman's 'bad gas,' said Sheriff Jerome Kramer." Apparently, the gas-attacked inmate had been complaining for a couple of days, and he'd even resorted to evasive maneuvers—which, in a small cell, amounted to staying at the other end. But since Bruggeman had continued to fart near him, he was eventually moved to a different cell at a safe distance from the fumes. Later that afternoon, Bruggeman sidled up to Dorris in the dinner line and let out a big one—resulting in a fight that left Dorris with a head injury. Sheriff Kramer blamed the fight on an overcrowded jailhouse, explaining, "When you've got a guy causing problems passing gas, there's no way to get away from the smell."

It was an airtight case.

So there you have it. The stories you have just read are true, and none of the names were changed to protect the innocent bystanders. As for the defendants, the verdict is in: "Gassy as charged!"

36

THE PRINCESS OF PASSIONATE GAS

For a certain type of American male caught in the grip of arrested development, the perfect girl is someone who's young, beautiful, fun, wickedly funny, and able to either drink or fart you under the table.

Could all these attributes really exist within one feminine body, or is this dream girl just that—a nighttime fantasy?

Well, I think I've found her, and you probably know her. She is Sarah Silverman, star of Comedy Central's *The Sarah Silverman Program* (2007–2009). I don't know if Sarah drinks, but she sure as hell can fart like a sailor—and proudly, too.

How can you not love a girl who, when asked by the *Chicago Sun-Times'* Mike Thomas what made her laugh, answered, "A well-placed fart joke tickles me. It is true that you can be the most cerebral comic in the world, but nothing's gonna make you laugh harder than a fart or something stupid."

In the first season of *The Sarah Silverman Program*, the sixth episode, called "Batteries," featured Sarah getting into a farting contest with her sister Laura and two neighbors at a coffee shop. Here's how Slate.com's Troy Patterson described it: "Soon, the four of them are sitting at the table, trading noisy farts. When it's Sarah's turn to deliver, she goes too far and accidentally poops her pants. After a musical interlude . . . she meets God, who answers her prayer that she might have that wind-passing moment back again ["a better fart" is what she wishes for], and then she's back at the brunch table, squeezing out a wicked but clean one. That seems like an awfully long way to go for a fart joke that would not pass muster in *Scary Movie 2*, but you've got to credit the sound designers for the way they make Silverman's juicy flatulence spurt out in stereo."

Wow!

The *Village Voice*'s Michael Musto, in a cover story interview titled "Sarah Silverman Is My Kind of Cunt" (and really, what other woman could you say that about in a major publication and be admiring when you said it?), addressed that same scene by asking her, "Which is the real Sarah—the crapper or the dreamer?" She answered, "I think I'm the crapper *and* the dreamer. It kills me that I fart and shit in an episode. I love aggressively stupid humor."

Another first-season episode called "Not Without My Daughter" required a particularly memorable fart, which one of Sarah's friends dropped in a police cruiser. Later, when he describes it on the phone as a "bomb," an electronic Homeland Security eavesdropper picks up the word—and the next thing he knows, he's being stunned with a Taser wielded by "men in black" and hauled off to an interrogation cell. That fart had to be a doozie, and in a voiceover track available on the first-season DVD, Sarah discusses it with her creative team, Rob Schab and Dan Sterling.

> Sterling: We listened to, I don't know, fifty different farts. In various combinations and resonances.
>
> Sarah: And they all had funny names.
>
> Rob: I spent a lot of time in the editing room, trying to fuse different farts together.

This isn't just some (gas) passing fad with Sarah. Way back in 1999, when SportsHollywood.com's Rodney Lee Conover asked her, "Which do you consider yourself first: actress, comedienne, writer, basketball player, or Hollywood Square?" she fired back, "Fart Machine."

How can you not love a girl who inspires the Parent's Television Council to damn her TV show as godless filth even as a Talmudic-scholar manqué named David Moscowitz is delivering a paean at the May 2009 National Commercial Association in San Diego called "Vernacular Narcissism, Jewish Postassimilation, and the Comedy of Sarah Silverman"?

Born (December 1, 1970) and raised in Bedford, New Hampshire, Silverman did her first stand-up gig in Boston when she was seventeen. Five years later she landed her first major comedy job, writing and performing on *Saturday Night Live.* That led to a steady succession of small roles on network TV (*Seinfeld*) and film (*There's Something About Mary*). She played a comedy writer on HBO's *The Larry Sanders Show* and an obsessed fan of detective Adrian Monk on A&E's *Monk.* She made outrageous phony phone calls on *Crank Yankers* and showcased her self-absorbed, guileless Jewish princess persona in her own film called *Jesus Is Magic* (2005). In the documentary *The Aristocrats,* which featured most of today's top comics trying to tell the world's dirtiest joke, Silverman managed to top everyone without losing her smile or the dark twinkle in her eyes.

Camille Dodero, writing in the *Village Voice* as a follow-up to Musto's piece, likened Sarah to Lenny Bruce and Richard Pryor because she tries to "find the outer boundary of the audience's tolerance and push beyond it, confronting and confusing the satisfied self-image of the liberal, sophisticated public." She can bend gender and ethnic stereotypes because she's pretty enough to get away with it *and* make the audience feel like it's in on the joke. Reviewing her Comedy Central show, the *Los Angeles Times* described her as "a Trojan horse of shock humor: cute and coquettish on the outside, brainy raunch if you get close . . . a Semitic goddess who is meaner and quicker, who can talk so dirty and yet be so pretty in cargo pants and a T-shirt." In the *New York Times,* Alessandra Stanley called her "innocently malevolent," and observed, "Ms. Silverman is as scatological as any young male comedian, relying on flatulence jokes and crude sexual remarks . . . [but] more slyly."

Naturally, a lot of people don't like her, don't get her, don't think she's pretty or funny—especially other women. One nonfan named Kimberly told Metacritic, "The only people who could possibly find [*The Sarah Silverman Program*] the least bit amusing are white trash folks who think fart jokes are funny and have absolutely zero class and no intelligence." On Jewlicious.com, blogger Beth wrote, "Sarah Silverman's irreverent I'm a pretty girl and can fart act is as irritating as my upstairs neighbors moving furniture at 11:50 p.m. on a weeknight."

But Beth was quickly overruled by blog-perv Uag's declaration, "If Sarah Silverman farted I would take the biggest whiff I have ever taken. . . . She's so sexy." Hey, you won't find any greater endorsement than that. When was the last time some guy wanted to smell a dainty poot from Roseanne?

———————————•

37

FARTY FACTOIDS ALL IN A ROW!

While researching this book, I stumbled onto all sorts of information, new and old, related to farting: little items, like the fact that Thomas Wolfe was angry because his editor, Max Perkins, cut the line "a fizzling and sulphuric fart" from his 1929 novel *Look Homeward, Angel*; that devout Jewish worshippers are prone to expelling gas while davening, especially after a long period of fasting; and that morticians vigorously massage a corpse's lower abdomen to release postmortem gas. Obviously these items don't merit more than a paragraph or two. So I've put them together into a chapter of bite-sized factoids, each one ready to be whipped out at a dinner party, on a tropical cruise, or in a Jacuzzi. Just remember to tell the folks where you got them.

1. According to the *Los Angeles Times*, when Art Whizin founded a successful chain of chili bowl–shaped Chili Bowl restaurants all over Los Angeles in the early 1930s, his slogan was, "We cook our beans backwards—you only get the hiccups." Whizin himself gets my vote as having the most suggestive last name for a guy who makes chili.

2. Britain's prolific postwar comic strip writer, Frank S. Pepper, gathered quotations from famous people in his later years and put them into a series of collections. In one book, called *20th Century Anecdotes*, he recalled a 1926 meeting at the Oxford Union between Winston Churchill and his

old friend and later Lord Chancellor, R. B. Haldane. Churchill tapped his portly pal's generous stomach and asked what he planned to call the baby. "If it's a boy, I'll call him George, after the king," Haldane said. "And if it's a girl I'll call her Mary. But if, as I strongly suspect, it is only wind, I shall call it Winston."

3. Chinese sculptor Chen Wen Ling's solo exhibition, "Emergency Exit," which opened at Beijing's Joyart Space in late August 2009, included a bronze Wall Street bull being propelled by a space-shuttle-like blast of flatulence coming from its ass and pinning the figure of ponzi-schemer Bernie Madoff against the wall with its horns. Called "What You See Might Not Be Real," the sculpture represents America's runaway economy goring Wall Street's greedy bingers.

4. Famous farters include Walt Disney (who not only farted frequently but was so indifferent to them that he'd fart in front of both men and women without comment, as if it were natural), President Lyndon Johnson (notorious), singer Tiny Tim (who confessed to eating a steady diet of beans, his favorite food), composer George Gershwin (who so suffered from chronic constipation that he valued every fart), Apple CEO Steve Jobs (known for really stinky ones, though he does try to hide the sound by ripping paper or clacking a stapler), pianist Glenn Gould (a hypochondriac who wrote voluminously of his gas problems), Whoopi Goldberg (why do you think her friends named her after a whoopee cushion?), and TV actress Jenny McCarthy (hot!).

5. I may have tracked down the worst fart on record. While reviewing Richard Fortey's memoirs about working in London's Natural History Museum in the *New York Review of Books*, Tim Flannery, himself a former curator and director for a museum in Sydney, Australia, recounted "the malodorous task of defleshing the whales that washed up" on the shore within what was called a stripping tank. "The whales arrive in all states of decay, and it's not unknown for them to become so full of gas as a result of internal decomposition that they literally explode, spraying foul greenish fluid in

all directions with great force. Warning is sometimes given by bursts of post-mortem flatulence . . . which seems able to carry the unique odor of rotting cetacean deep into one's pores, mouth, and nasal cavity."

6. According to the October 24, 2008, issue of the journal *Science*, one of the stink factors in farts can help fight high blood pressure. Amelia Tomas reported that researchers at Johns Hopkins in Baltimore found that cells lining the blood vessels of mice produce hydrogen sulfide (H_2S), the rotten-egg-smelling gas that helps give flatulence its smell, and that this action lowers the rodents' blood pressure by relaxing the blood vessels. This gas is "no doubt" produced in cells lining human blood vessels too, the researchers said. "Now that we know hydrogen sulfide's role in regulating blood pressure, it may be possible to design drug therapies that enhance its formation as an alternative to the current methods of treatment for hypertension," said neuroscientist and medical doctor Solomon H. Snyder, who coauthored the *Science* study.

7. According to Scribd.com, Colorado's Department of Revenue–Division of Motor Vehicles recently nixed the following vanity license plate applications: FART, FARTEN, FARTIN, FARTN, OLDFRT, OLFART, and PASSGAS.

8. On March 8, 2008, inventors Travis Grigsby, Steven Michael Miller, and Lisa Anne Seacat, on behalf of International Business Machines (IBM), applied for a U.S. patent for an invention that "enliven[s] conference calls" by injecting prerecorded sound effects whenever the conversation drops into an awkward pause or falls silent. The device will first monitor a company's phone lines to determine acceptable periods of silence within that company, and then, once it sets a dead air limit, will suddenly play audio gags, including farts and noises or voices specific to the company, to let the callers know that time's a-wastin' on the boss's dime. According to the application, "If interjections (e.g., laughs, cheers, or jingles), and the like, could be made during the conference call at times of boredom, the conference call may be enlivened and more interesting for the participants."

9. We've all heard of ayatollahs and mullahs issuing *fatwas*, or *fatwahs*—legal religious edicts against individuals and behaviors. The most infamous, and extreme, was the Iranian Ayatollah Khomeini's 1989 call to Muslims world-wide that they had a religious duty to murder Salman Rushdie for writing the "blasphemous" novel *The Satanic Verses*. Iran's religious leaders rescinded the fatwa in 1998, after Khomeini's death. But what about a *faswa*? In Arabic that's a silent fart, and you don't have to be a mullah or an ayatollah to issue faswas all the time. However, thanks to the Arabic diet of spicy lamb, dates, and figs, most farts in that part of the world are hardly silent, which means that locals have kept their faswas to a minimum. More common is the *eefessy* (silent but deadly). A regular Arabic fart is a *fasia*, followed by its *fesa* (stink). Other types of fart besides the *faswa* are the *eegayas* or *zirt* (loud) and *eezarat* (soft). In Richard Burton's nineteenth-century translation of *The Arabian Nights*, a king in "The Tale of Ali Nur el-Din and Miriam" called his son Fasyan, which means farter. In any event, though Arabs consider a belch to be an acceptable form of appreciation for a good meal, they take great offense when someone delivers a *faswa* in their presence.

10. For the last forty years of his life, naturalist Charles Darwin (1809–1882), whose *On the Origin of Species* brought evolution into the cultural main-stream, was either a serious hypochondriac or a very sick man. He was often so debilitated that just day-to-day activity, much less intellectual and sci-entific inquiry, exhausted him. Among his ailments were vomiting, cramps, colics, and really bad farting, which he often called "baddish," "sharp," or "excessive." According to *The Correspondence of Charles Darwin*, he described his maladies to a friend in an 1865 letter: "For 25 years extreme spasmodic daily & nightly flatulence: occasional vomiting, on two occasions prolonged during months. . . . Now vomiting & every paroxysm of flatulence." In a January 3, 1866, letter to Dr. Bence Jones, Darwin lamented that "on most days 3 hours after luncheon or dinner I have . . . bad flatulence lasting to the next meal. I forgot to say that taking the whole day, the flatulence is some-what diminished especially on my better days." Oftentimes, according to biographer Keith Francis, "Wrenching stomach aches with fits of flatulence

made Darwin too embarrassed to leave his house." He sometimes stayed in bed for months and consulted with at least twenty doctors over the years without getting a proper diagnosis of what ailed him.

11. When twenty-nine-year-old Mexican pop singer and telenova actress Lucero performed at an internationally televised concert in Chile in 1994, she ended one of her hit songs, put her hands behind her back and bowed to the massive audience. Her microphone happened to be in the hand closest to her derriere when the bending movement caused her to fart loudly. Perhaps her internationally famous 1986 album, *Un Pedacito De Mi* ("a little piece of me") should have been called *Un Pedocito De Mi* ("my little fart").

12. If you think you have farting problems now, just wait till you have gastrointestinal surgery, such as gastric bypass or bariatric surgery, to lose a large amount of weight you otherwise can't get rid of. Gastric bypass makes the stomach smaller and allows food to detour around part of the intestine, whereas bariatric surgery alters the digestive process, but they both restrict the body's absorption of calories and nutrients. That means that if you plan on being *The Biggest Loser*, you're going to have to live with farting—really stinky farting—at a new level of intensity (something the NBC reality show doesn't dramatize). When food that normally would have been digested in the stomach reaches the colon with its nutrients still intact, the enzymes and bacteria down there go into a feeding frenzy. It's like the peasants who suddenly become best friends with the king and hang out at the palace table, gorging themselves on wine and lamb and tossing greasy, half-eaten turkey drumsticks over their shoulders. And *ohhh!* (or *oy!* if you're so inclined), the gas! Nothing can really stop it, and post-op patients often have to change their routines to avoid embarrassing social situations.

13. As bizarre as this next story sounds, to the best of my knowledge it's true. It was reported by the Danish news agency B.T. (bt.dk/nyheder) on April 12, 2002. According to reporter Leif Hansen, a thirty-year-old surgery patient named Jorgen Olsen created a small air blast that scorched his buttocks and genitals. A resident of tiny Hammershøj on Denmark's Jutland

Peninsula, Olsen went into Viborg-Kjellerup Hospital in nearby Kjellerup (now part of Silkeborg) for what he thought would be a small operation. He ended up staying for six weeks. "When I woke up after surgery [on February 13] it was immediately with severe pain in the buttocks, among other things," Olsen told Hansen. (I'm quoting the Google translation; and no, Olsen and Hansen aren't a comedy team.) Olsen had gone into the hospital to have a fistula, or abscess, removed from his rectum. (No, this isn't the old "abscess makes the fart go *honda* joke.") To seal off the small blood vessels, Dr. Jørn Ulrik Kristensen used an electrical instrument to cauterize them. At the same time, an attending nurse swabbed the area around Olsen's bottom with liquid disinfectant, which happened to be flammable. "There must have been a glow from the operation in the vicinity," said Dr. Kristensen, because Olsen let an exceptionally gassy flatus—a *prut*, as the Danish call it—whose methane and hydrogen sulfide content must have been considerable. Suddenly the electrical instrument set off both the disinfectant and Olsen's fart, creating "what appeared a flashover around the patient's lower parts," Kristensen told Hansen. The patient later said there were no permanent injuries beyond a few red scars. I should point out that the folks at Snopes.com who investigate urban legends have not completely confirmed the veracity of this story, even though it came from a major news outlet, but they don't discount it either.

14. The stinkiest spice in the world may also be an anti-fart remedy. According to the *Hindu*, India's national newspaper, *asafetida* is great not just for keeping insects away from plants but also for flavoring food and fending off flatulence. A resinous gum from the root of three kinds of plants of the Ferula family (a cousin of the carrot), asafetida got its name from the Persian word *asa*, or resin, and the Latin word *foetida*, better known in modern English as the origin of *fetid*, or rotten smelling. That's because it smells like a mixture of manure and overcooked cabbage until it's heated, and then it smells like onions and garlic—all thanks to its sulfides-heavy composition. Europeans generally call asafetida "devil's dung" or "devil's shit" (for example, it's *merde du diable* in French). Indians have used it since

ancient times, but they must keep it in airtight containers so that its stench doesn't affect other spices on their shelves.

It seems ironic, then, that asafetida is also a great antidote to flatulence, because its ingredients reportedly reduce gas-producing microflora in the stomach and disturb the gas-producing carbonic anhydrase enzyme in the intestine. Indians not only use it as a common condiment for lentils and beans, but also paste a small raw chunk on infants' belly buttons to relieve colic. According to Online Health Care, "Asafetida is commonly used to treat bloating and gas to prevent flatulence, but it also quells stomach cramps, eases indigestion, and relieves constipation."

15. "Big Chicken Mushroom invents a suppository that silences farts!" If that headline doesn't strain your credulity, read on. According to the Fashion Finds column at Inventor Spot, a creative prankster-inventor in Wuhan, China, who calls himself Big Chicken Mushroom (perhaps something got garbled in the translation) has apparently redesigned a plastic toothbrush-carrying tube by cutting off one end and punching small holes in the other—or at least that's what it looks like. It's called the Ultimate Fart Silencer. If you think you're going to be gassy, you insert the four-inch tube, open end first, into your butt (ideally in a private moment). Later, when you fart, the holes near the exit will diffuse the gas silently, because the tube is keeping the fatty flaps and folds of your integument—the brown membrane at the anal entrance—from noisily vibrating against each other. Mr. Mushroom (I don't known him well enough to call him Big Chicken) also suggests that for special occasions you first put a scented cotton ball in the plastic tube before inserting it; that way, he says, your fart will smell like flowers (or perhaps stink like those gagging-sweet "air fresheners" in public urinals). There's a video demonstration of how to use the silencer on YouTube, but if you later need an emergency-room explanation of how and why it got stuck up your butt, you're on your own.

There you have it: fifteen topics for scintillating conversations. Now you're ready to be the life of that Thanksgiving family dinner or office Christmas party.

38

STRAIGHT POOP ON THE YOOP!

All around America there are many regional subcultures whose geographic and social isolation, ethnic makeup, and singular history make each a world unto itself. There are Appalachian hillbillies, Carolina-Georgia Gullahs, Louisiana Cajuns, Yoopers . . . Yoopers?

Ya, da Yoopers. Dat's dem all right, eh? And to hear dem talk about it, da Yoopers love to fart.

Okay, geographic and social isolation? Check. Yoopers live in Michigan's Upper Peninsula, or U.P. (pronounced "Yoop"), a land bridge that arches from northern Wisconsin to Ontario, Canada, without even touching the oven-mitt-shaped landmass we think of as Michigan. The U.P. and the rest of the state are separated by giant lakes, and the only thing that joins them is the Mackinac Bridge, located at the only point where they get within a few miles of each other. The U.P. contains nearly a third of Michigan's land area, but the 328,000 Yoopers make up only 3 percent of its total population, creating a strong regional identity that's about as far from downstate Detroit and Kalamazoo as you can get. The Yoopers' idea of a metropolis is Marquette, population just under twenty thousand. The cultural center is Escanaba, home to thirteen thousand.

Ethnic identity? Check. Most of the Yoopers are of Scandinavian and French Canadian ancestry, but the most common nationality seems to be

Finnish, a group that even other Scandinavians consider strange. (Consider that Finnish and Hungarian are the only major European languages that don't come from a common Indo-European source; plus, nobody's quite sure where Finlanders originated.) There's only a handful of counties in the United States that have more residents of Finnish descent than of any other, and they all happen to be in the U.P.

History? Check. With a wintry climate and bad soil conspiring against any serious agricultural enterprise, there's not much in the U.P. but boondocks. Logging and mining are the only major industries.

So what kind of subculture has this area created? Consider that many Yoopers think of themselves more as Yoopers than Michiganders and call the rest of their fellow state citizens Trolls, because they live "below da bridge"—the aforementioned Mackinac Bridge. Yoopers in the westernmost counties are even in a different time zone from everyone else. There are no freeways and only a snippet of I-75, so driving the six hundred miles down to Detroit is a full day's journey.

When some Yoopers talk, they sound somewhere between those Canadian hosers, the McKenzie Brothers—on the old *SCTV* program—and the Minnesota locals in the film *Fargo*. "Dat's a pretty good fart, eh?" "Eh, you betcha." Because they're down-home and proud of it, their jokes tend to be self-deprecating, peopled with good-hearted yokels with Finnish names: "Toivo and Eino decide to drive down to da Motor City. When dey get across da bridge dey see a sign dat reads DETROIT LEFT, so dey turn around and go home."

You get the idea.

The U.P.'s most famous tourist attraction is Mackinac Island, a resort hotel trapped in Victorian amber, where the 1980 Jane Seymour and Christopher Reeve romance *Somewhere in Time* was filmed. But the real Yooper tourist trap is Da Yoopers Tourist Trap about 120 miles west, at Ishpeming, on U.S. 41 West. This is the spot for all those folks who believe that the "authentic" Yooper lifestyle entails farting, belching, drinking Bosch beer, telling jokes about big asses and outhouses (usually together), and fishing and hunting (usually without catching anything, but who cares as long as there's plenty of beer and fellow Yoopers). (As you might have guessed, a lot of this is good-natured leg-pulling. Yoopers, like my fellow West Virginia "hillbillies," come in all classes, from rich to poor, and many resent the oafish caricatures that have popped up in media folklore. But others have a lot of fun with them.) Da Yoopers Tourist Trap, out front near the highway, has a giant red sign advertising the technological wonder of "two flushing toilets" (Yoopers call indoor commodes "one-holers") and the world's largest (twenty-three feet long) working chainsaw, Big Gus, along with a giant, truck-mounted shotgun, Big Ernie, that was actually fired once, but the recoil of sending a rock wrapped in duct tape more than two miles away into a corn field knocked it off its perch and broke some windows besides. But best of all, the Tourist Trap contains an extensive gift shop with its own little potty section in back, featuring farting doorbells, farting pens, cans of "fish assholes," turd necklaces, and any number of other gadgets and jokes. "Farting is big business here," says Anna Gully, who runs the gift shop and is quoted on the Roadside America website. "Farting in general sells." Out back there are two shithouse props—Da 2-Holer and Da Dorkmeister Outhouse—where tourists can say "cheese" as they stick their heads through the holes for a photo op.

The shop also sells CDs by a local rock 'n' roll band called Da Yoopers, whose dozen-plus albums on their own You Guys label include the masterpiece *Songs for Fart Lovers*, with a list of titles that reads like the chapters in my books. "She Loves to Fart" and the tender ballad "Pucker and Smell" are the highlights, but there's also "No One Here to Fart On," "If She Farts on the First Date (She's a Keeper)," "I Never Hear My Mom Fart," and "You're My Favorite Turd." However, if you're looking for their fabled "Football Fart Fandango," that's on another album. Da Yoopers tour around the Midwest, playing their tunes and telling Yooper jokes. Their recording of "The Second Week of Deer Camp," a tale of endless drinking and farting, was actually a hit all over Michigan and in parts of surrounding states.

Da Yoopers also solicit farts from their many (mostly male) fans for possible use on future albums. As they say on their DaYoopers.com website, the band wants real farts, not fake ones like "the armpit farts, the lip farts, whoopy cushion farts or those synthesized lame attempts." They want the gassers "born of Aunt Helga's double baked bean casserole, nurtured in [a] beer and pickled egg environment, hanging around until the peak of potency, earth busting eruptions of joy. The kind that make the guys at camp high-five and the kind little Harold sings about in the new song 'If I Could Fart Like My Dad.' Be proud, make 'em loud and record them for future generations' enjoyment. . . . Hold the microphone 4 to 6 inches away . . . and let 'er rip."

Another Yoopers website asks such questions as "Do Women Fart?" and get answers like: "[A]ll I have to say is my wife has a big fat ass that sends out monster air bombs. I mean she keeps right up with me and as loud as they are, they seldom stink, although once in a while [she] farts raw sewage." Another writer disagreed, saying, "Hell no!!! They can't keep their mouths shut long enough to build any back pressure." But then a real Yooper steps in with: "Da answer is, ya dey do. I grew up in da U.P. in Marquette, living wit my parents. My dad would let one [of] his go anytime, and my ma would overpower him wit one [of] her farts. She could empty a room out at da camp and dats pretty bad, eh? My sis is just as bad too. She would come up to me and say, 'eh Jim, got a present for ya,' I'd say, 'oh ya' and she would let a juicy one out dat made my nose hairs curl."

One of the best-known Yoopers is actually only an honorary member, actor Jeff Daniels, who's a Troll from Chelsea, just outside Ann Arbor. But he's a big fan of deer camp bonding and flatulence. Not long after he shared plenty of toilet gags with costar Jim Carrey in 1994's *Dumb and Dumber*, Daniels wrote a Yooper-dialect play called *Escanaba in da Moonlight* that ran at Detroit's Gem Theater for well over a year. He filmed *Escanaba in da Moonlight* as a small indie in 2001, which inspired Yooper reviewer "Tom Sawyer" to write on the movie's Internet Movie Database page that "[my wife and I] thought it was funny. Especially the fart jokes. Sorry ladies, but I am a hunter and have been in more than a few deer camps to know what actually goes on. They play cards, fart, drink, tell jokes, read *Playboy* magazines in the john and tell all kinds of stories."

Daniels has since staged two prequels, *Escanaba in Love* in 2001 and *Escanaba* in 2009, to complete a trilogy. One of the running gags in all three plays is that anyone guilty of farting has to drop a penny into the Gas Jar. Actor Jack McCord, who played the lead character, Albert Soady, in *Escanaba*, told Adrianne DeWeese of the Independence [Missouri] *Examiner*, "This is a manly man play. You'll see churly men in their underwear. When the Mrs. brings the man out to a night of theater and he moans, well, this is the play he'll want to see." Costar Kevin Elmore, who plays his son, chimed in with, "While the play has lots of crude humor and jokes, it's a story about family and dedication. And maybe a little flatulence."

But in the end, Da Yoopers get the last word on defining the Yooper nerd with the song "Why Do Girls Think I'm Scary."

If I had a girl friend
You know my love would never end
I'd buy her gifts, I'd buy her things
I'd buy her pearls and diamond rings
I'd lose some weight, I'd exercise
And if I'd fart, I'd apologize . . .
Why do girls think I'm scary?
I wish somebody knew
Why do girls think I'm scary?
Why do they act like I smell like poo?
Or is it because when I pass wind
It smells just like burnt shoe?
Why do girls think I'm scary?
I don't know, maybe you do.

39

NETHER WINDS IN THE NETHERLANDS!

The pharmaceutical industry bombards Americans with ads for prescription drugs that cure erectile dysfunction, depression, high cholesterol, toenail fungus, and other accretions of advancing age. The message is always rather contradictory: as we watch, say, a handsome middle-aged couple frolicking through the marigolds enjoying the effects of some miracle drug, a disclaiming, rapid-fire voice in the background lists possible unfrolicksome side effects, like erectile dysfunction, heart attack, dry mouth, bad gas, insomnia—"And tell your doctor if you're having obsessive thoughts of suicide." Though the "cures" sound worse than the maladies, these ads must be working, because Big Pharma continues to spend hundreds of millions of dollars on them each year, and TV viewers keep medicating themselves by demanding prescriptions from their doctors. We've come a long way since the days when the family physician decided what the patient needed—but then again, corporations do a vastly more compassionate job of taking care of us.

In Holland the government has banned all direct, American-style pharmaceutical huckstering, but the pill conglomerates work around this restriction by running so-called "symptom-disease" ads. "Pharmacists may not advertise prescription-only drugs," the Amsterdam-based TV show *Radar* reported. "They therefore frequently launch campaigns aimed at the medical condition itself." It's the same tactic used by American political-action groups: legally constrained by campaign spending limits from attacking a rival candidate, they pour unlimited money instead into attacking his political position in so-called "phony issue ads" without naming him. That's why, in late summer of 2009, *Radar* decided to expose these drug companies—with flatulence, or as the Dutch call it, *winderigheid*.

It all began when the Dutch Healthcare Inspectorate reported that online medical websites were violating the ban on prescription drug advertising. Twenty-seven of the forty-one websites they checked were promoting specific medicine brands by name.

The producers of *Radar*, a TROS network ombudsman program, decided to see if they could prank the pharmaceutical spin doctors into perpetrating anti-fart-pill campaigns. First they hired the country's most respected market research company, TNS-NIPO, to help their fictitious Client Consulting Company set up a website survey at Hetluchtop.nl to see if people were having farting problems. "I suffer from gas daily" was a typical statement to be checked Yes or No. Within a couple of weeks, over 17,500 people had taken the test. TNS-NIPO, unaware of the ruse, tallied the results and announced that 25 percent of Netherlanders experienced more farting than they thought was normal or necessary. The report seemed fairly innocuous. Everybody breaks wind (*alle een wind laten*), and everybody goes through periods when they *een wind laten* too much and perhaps at the wrong time. Big deal: farts (*scheten*) happen. Nothing to get worried about, right?

TNS-NIPO gave the survey results maximum exposure. And as health-related websites and radio programs began reproducing the data, they trumpeted the country's "excessive flatulence" as a serious health issue and helpfully guided viewers to specific drugs that might mitigate this national scourge—not as unlawful advertising, mind you, but as "fair comment" within concerned "news" reports and articles about the serious national flatulence problem. Most of these sites, as you might expect, were surreptitiously owned by pharmaceuticals. Dutch journalists, who were quick to exploit the farting angle, borrowed the information without checking on its reliability or its sources and kept the windmills turning.

Radar exposed these findings on Monday, August 31, 2009, both on the air (with host Antoinette Hertsenberg) and online. "Drug Manufacturers will use the media to sell as many pills as possible," said the Trosradar.nl website, adding that the media unwittingly helped them. For Hertsenberg it "was amazing to see how easy and uncritical" reporters were. For example, one story by ANP, the Netherlands' top news agency, began with the line: "One in four Dutch people are gassier than the average," and continued with "Changing your . . . diet may help, but there are also drugs [that prevent gassiness]."

Radar's exposé wasn't unexpected. Three days earlier, one pharma-friendly website, MedicalFacts.nl, tried to defuse *Radar*'s upcoming bomb-shell with an article headlined (in the English translation): "Hetluchtop.nl, Website for Flatulence, a Hoax." According to writer Janine Budding, "This website is an absolute nonsense test. . . . They have left a breeze [*een wind hebben gelaten*, which also means 'they have farted']." Bunning noted that the company behind the website "is not registered at the Chamber nor to the address given on the site. Indeed, the company is not registered at all. . . . That really exceeds the limits of ethics." Feigning outrage, Budding went on to call *Radar*'s underhanded methods worse than what it was accusing the medical companies of doing and branded its "cut and paste journalism . . . shameless news."

Budding followed up on the day of the big broadcast with another Medical Facts broadside, claiming that *Radar*'s accusations were wrong. She argued that even though flatulence may normally be "a symptom of disorders like indigestion and irritable bowel," more extreme cases "associated with weight loss, severe abdominal pain or bleeding during bowel movement may indicate a more serious condition. In that case it is advisable to seek medical advice"... and to get a prescription for a drug.

Because severe flatulence can also damage one's social life and general well-being, Budding played the political correctness card by claiming that *Radar*'s irreverent tone ridiculed gas sufferers. Then she got to the point she wanted to make: "There are several medications with strong wind as mild side effects. The pharmacists about which we consulted provided us a list of sixty-six drugs that have gas or flatulence as an undesirable effect." Among the best-known of these drugs was Metformin.

There it was, the real message—just as *Radar* had said. Medical Facts had slipped in a word from one of its sponsors. There's even a footnote: "Gastrointestinal adverse effects including Flatulence occur in about 30% of patients during initiation of Metformin therapy," followed by a long list of possible side effects and how to mitigate them by regulating the dosage of Metformin. It was reverse-psychology advertising. Sure, this drug may make you fart, but you can control it by not taking so much.

In the end, *Radar* pissed off the pharmaceuticals, the doctors, the news media, and even its unwitting partner, TNS NIPO, which issued a September 1 statement denying that it knew anything about the hoax it had helped perpetrate; at the same time it defended the methodology of the "serious survey" and the results "show[ing] that for several million Dutch, excessive flatulence is a problem."

Who knew that farting could create such a huge cloud of controversy— not to mention even more profits for corporations?

40

BABY, LET'S GO DUTCH!

Despite the growing acceptance of farting in American culture today, there's still one place where it remains under the covers. And that's under the covers. Maybe you're sound asleep or just kind of dozing off or lost in a book with your head sunk comfortably in the pillow. You're as unsuspecting as a lamb. Suddenly the person lying in bed next to you lays a really stinky egg, grabs the bedspread or the blanket that's on top of both of you, and pulls it tightly over your head, shouting, "Dutch oven! Dutch oven!" The dank, brimstone atmosphere that left your lover's innards only moments earlier is now all around you, the air that you breathe, so oppressive you can't help but think—if you're still able to form a clear thought— that the local SWAT team must have tossed a turd gas grenade into your bedroom.

It's easy to see how the so-called Dutch-oven fart got its name. A real Dutch oven is a large cook pot (of plain or enameled cast iron) that steams food, with its heavy lid trapping all the heat and moisture and flavor and aroma inside. Dutch ovens come in various sizes, small to large, designed for either indoor or campfire cooking. American companies have been manufacturing them since the 1800s. There are dozens of Dutch oven cookbooks and far more chefs who wouldn't think of cooking any other way.

And then there's the Dutch oven where what's steaming is you. If the covers are heavy enough, and your partner's grip and body weight are heavy enough, you're steeping in an airtight underworld of swamp gas.

There's even a "rolling Dutch oven," where the driver farts in the car, rolls up all the electric windows and, to complete the effect, turns on the heater full blast. But the bedroom variety is the worst, simply because that's the place that's supposed to be your refuge from the world, not your gas chamber.

Let me say right now that the Dutch oven—the one in the bedroom, not the kitchen—should not be confused with a "Dutch treat." A Dutch treat is going fifty-fifty on a bill. A Dutch oven can be fifty-fifty if the farter wants to join the fun under the covers, but it usually doesn't work that way. Ignore those who call their Dutch ovens Dutch treats, because they don't know what they're talking about.

The very intimacy of the act determines that a Dutch oven is likely perpetrated by a longtime lover. Because roommates or newlyweds generally take a while before they dare break wind in front of each other, the relationship must have settled into true familiarity if someone feels comfortable enough to share butt gas with the other in its full, rotten intensity—and maniacally laugh about it while screaming, "Dutch oven! Dutch oven!"

Radio's Dr. Laura Schlessinger would probably say the romance has gone out of the relationship, or perhaps love has gone stale—especially if you're getting mugged by the muggy magumbo on Valentine's Day. That goes double if the perpetrator first let several nasty sulfuric air bubbles build up a head of steam and *then* threw the covers over your head and held you down for more than thirty seconds. At that point a Dutch oven may qualify as grounds for either a divorce or a restraining order.

Outside of David Cross gassing his TV "wife" Portia di Rossi on Fox's *Arrested Development* and farty Fred Willard pulling a blanket over himself and three other people in the epic 2007 failure *Epic Movie*, onscreen Dutch ovens are rare. You'll have to go to England to watch a TV commercial for Warmup, a home heating system installer, that shows an older man giving his sleeping wife a Dutch oven, as the words, "Even a cold bastard needs a warm home" appear on the screen. On second thought, you can just stay home and log onto the Internet, where YouTube presents an endless succession of gagging and giggling husbands, wives, lovers, buddies, and strange bedfellows as they stifle and smother one another in blanketed hothouses unfit for the most sturdy orchids. In fact, you could probably watch video Dutch ovens all day long and never see the same one twice.

It's amazing that couples are so willing to let a world of strangers into their bedrooms—but under their covers, too? That really stinks.

41

HOW BAD WAS IT?

When guys talk about their most notorious farts, it's important that they describe the aftereffects. Creativity is a plus when describing these air benders—yes, I said air benders—rippers so powerful they make the air shimmer like a desert mirage. But when you recount their impact, the effects should be humorous, and devastating, but more than anything they must suggest the corrosive and sulfuric powers of a Fartzilla. Here are ten thumbnail descriptions that will enhance your own story of that most memorable fart:

1. I could taste it.
2. It peeled the wallpaper.
3. The goldfish went belly-up.
4. The fire alarm went off.
5. The dog died.
6. I couldn't feel my legs.
7. My asshole apologized and tried to suck it back in.
8. Neighbors came over and asked if we were having boiled owl for dinner.
9. Several federal agents in Hazmat suits showed up and tented the house.
10. The local paper mill sued me for pain and suffering.

42

THE DAY HIS BUTT WENT PSYCHO

Among the many synonyms for fart are "butt bomb," "butt blast," and "ass detonation," all suggesting an explosive release of gas that compels bystanders to shout something like, "Man, did you just blow your guts out?" Flatulence has always inspired bombshell bombast. One comes from the arse, the other from the arsenal. Medieval munitions makers even named the petard—the old bell-shaped, gunpowder-filled blockbuster that Shakespeare enshrined in Hamlet's line, "For 'tis the sport to have the engineer / hoist with his own petard"—after the French and Middle English word *pet*, or fart (from the Latin *peditum*). But who knew that Al-Qaeda terrorists were going to take the idea of a butt bomb seriously?

According to Stratfor Global Intelligence, a Texas-based private services firm, Prince Mohammed bin Nayef, Saudi Arabia's deputy interior minister who heads the desert kingdom's counterterrorism campaign, was holding a public gathering on Friday evening, August 28, 2009, as part of the celebration of Ramadan, the Islamic month of fasting and prayer. One person who came to talk to the prince was Abdullah Hassan Taleh al-Asiri, a known Al-Qaeda operative who had told Prince Nayef in advance that he wanted to give himself up, renounce terrorism, repent to Allah for his sins, and be admitted into Nayef's amnesty and rehabilitation program for jihadis. Nayef, who had already converted several former

Al-Qaeda militants, saw al-Asiri's renunciation as yet another coup in his war against the terrorist organization. Al-Asiri had surrendered in Yemen on Thursday and spent the next thirty hours in custody as he was transported by private jet to Nayef's palace in Jedda. Security men had already checked him for explosives and weapons several times by the time they ushered him into a small room where the prince was waiting. At that point an outside accomplice with a cell phone detonated a three- or four-inch-long bomb that al-Asiri had hidden where the sun don't shine.

The blast literally blew his ass off, along with most of his other lower body parts. Prince Nayef was unharmed but shaken up. In a strange way, Shakespeare's analogy had been partly played out. "Hoist with his own petard" means the maker is figuratively thwarted by his own devilish device. Hamlet, knowing that his stepfather, King Claudius, was sending him off to England to be murdered, avoided his fate by sending the king's dupes, Rosencrantz and Guildenstern, in his place with a sealed order of execution. And now, an anonymous Al-Qaeda bomb maker had sent al-Asiri in *his* place. In both cases the mechanics' ultimate designs were foiled and the carriers ended up as the victims, though al-Asiri was certainly a willing (if unsuccessful) one. (I just hope his seventy-two virgins in paradise don't start whispering and snickering to each other, "He's got no ass!") The main difference was that Prince Hamlet ultimately outsmarted the mechanic, whereas Prince Nayef was just plain lucky.

International security experts, including Stratfor, immediately grasped its deeper implications. The terrorists had used their first "keister bomb." Keister (pronounced "*kee*-ster") is a nineteenth-century underworld German or Yiddish term for bag or satchel that was later generalized to mean the anal cavity, probably because prisoners and their visitors used it to carry drugs and crude weapons past jailers. By the 1980s it was a verb, "to keister."

Covering the story for the *Kansas City Star*, reporter Rick Montgomery asked Paul Worsey of the Missouri University of Science and Technology whether we should worry about keister bombers. Worsey thought the threat was overblown, saying, "The force of such an explosion would be in the direction of the easiest exit. The rest of the body would work like a sandbag against the blast . . . though it would be a mess."

But Stratfor analysts disagree: "The surprise was complete and the Saudis did not see the attack coming—the operation could have succeeded had it been better executed. . . . It is quite likely that [Al-Qaeda] failed to do adequate testing with the device and did not know what its effective kill radius was." If al-Asiri had had in his possession the means of setting off the bomb when he wanted, and had turned his back to the prince at the moment of detonation, he would have fulfilled his mission. Or perhaps if the bomb had been bigger—though that would certainly be a *stretch*, especially during the thirty hours prior to the blast. Ouch!

By early September 2009, CBS News was speculating how easy it would be for a keister bomber to get on an airplane and blow it up. All it would take would be a ticket for a window seat where he could press his buttocks against the bulkhead and—boom! Stratfor's analysts wrote that even a small keister bomb "would likely have a catastrophic result . . . especially if it were removed from the bomber's body and placed in a strategic location on board the aircraft." Andrea McCauley, a spokeswoman for the federal Transportation Security Administration in Dallas, tried to allay fears raised by these scenarios by saying, "We have a lot of different layers of security in place." And Lewis Page, a science writer for the British online journal the *Register*, likewise called for level heads: "Don't get anyone's bowels in an uproar." But if a bomber has a tube of plastic explosives (Semtex or PETN) with no attached metal parts up his butt, how is airport security going to find it? Let's face it, even though passengers have willingly acquiesced to removing their shoes and divesting themselves of bottled liquids in response to previous Al-Qaeda tactics, will they consent to security screeners giving them the ol' proctology poke?

Flying the friendly skies shouldn't be *that* friendly!

43

THIS IS YOUR BRAIN ON GAS!

Neologisms—newly coined words and phrases—come and go, but occasionally one so perfectly fits what everyone's talking about that it spreads like a virus into the national vocabulary. One such term is *brainfart*, or *brain fart*. (We'll have to work that out; to be fully functional it needs one standard spelling, so for now I'll use one word.) Back in 1998, when I was writing *Who Cut the Cheese?*, I described a brainfart in passing as "an American college expression for a sudden loss of memory; it has evolved among Internet users to mean a mistake created by a mental glitch."

Since then the brainfart has been turning up everywhere. For young people, it's the "D'oh!" moment, that dumb thought that pops into your head long enough for you to stupidly act on it, after which you shamefacedly ask yourself, "What the hell was I thinking?" For example, Britney Spears, regretting her latest brunette look, told the press, "I was having a huge brainfart when I did the dark hair. My hairdresser persuaded me." On a slight variation, it can be a sudden loss of verbal coherency, as when Dublin actor Colin Farrell, discussing the art of improvisation, told the *Independent*'s Leslie Felperin in 2003, "Every now and then you have a brainfart, you know, something [stupid] will come out of your mouth."

For middle-age people, especially the baby boomers, brainfart perfectly describes the loss of memory bits that has them searching the tips of their tongues for the name of their best friend, that actor on their favorite TV show, or the restaurant where they ate just an hour ago. Old folks have for some time called these ditherings "senior moments," but aging boomers will have nothing to do with any expression that links them to "senior citizens." The hip-sounding brainfart comes to the rescue.

For folks in between, especially those who spend lots of time on computers, "I just had a brainfart" replaces "I just lost my train of thought." They've also adopted the idea that their computers have brainfarts—glitches that inexplicably disrupt the orderly flow of ones and zeroes.

You can find the word *brainfart* in family newspapers, as when the *San Francisco Examiner* in 2009 headlined a "Brain Fart Trivia" contest being held at the famous Lookout restaurant every Wednesday night.

It showed up in a mainstream film as early as 1997, in an exchange between Demi Moore and Scott Wilson in *G.I. Jane*. Wilson, playing her commanding officer, asked Moore's character, "Did you just have a brainfart, Lieutenant?"

"Begging your pardon, sir?" she said.

"Did you just waltz in here and bark at your commanding officer?" he asked. "Because if you did, I would call that a bona fide brainfart, and I resent it when people fart in my office."

In 2005 Canadian TV even featured a full-length movie called *Brain Fart,* featuring rap and rock stars (including 50 Cent, Billie Joe Armstrong of Green Day, and the Backstreet Boys) and adding clever quips to popular music videos, à la VH1's much more clever *Pop-Up Videos* show.

Amateur etymologists guess that *brainfart* sprang from *brainstorm*, its opposite, sometime in the early 1980s. A brainstorm gives you ideas; a brainfart gets in the way of an idea. A brainstorm makes your eyes light up like a bloody crime scene doused with Luminol; a brainfart gives you a murder victim's blank stare. For your mental slip to truly be cranial flatulence, however, you're expected to recover fairly quickly and realize you've just had a brainfart, accompanied either by blurting out an announcement ("Uh oh, *brainfart!*")

or an apology ("Sorry, I just had a brainfart"). If you don't realize it happened, you may be brain dead . . . or slipping into dementia.

There's a Mr. Brainfart: Denis Gauthier, a much-traded, hot-headed hockey defense player who at last report was an L.A. King. Gauthier earned his "honorific sobriquet," says Wikipedia, because he "momentarily loses his sense of logic . . . and does something dumb" as a matter of course.

Wikipedia also claims that there's a Dr. Brainfart, neuroscientist Tom Eichele of Haukeland University Hospital at the University of Bergen in Norway. Dr. Eichele has been studying brain lapses using functional Magnetic Resonance Imaging (fMRI), which can display cognitive functions happening in real time by scanning the brain. In 2008 Dr. Eichele and his associates, writing in the journal *Proceedings of the National Academy of Sciences*, claimed that they could detect a "maladaptive brain activity change" up to thirty seconds before it happened. But when I contacted him by email, Dr. Eichele told me that he never used the word *brainfart* in any of his papers. "This is something that came up in some of the press coverage and apparently made it to a Wikipedia entry," he said, unappreciative of the Dr. Brainfart honorific.

On the Internet, the word *brainfart* is everywhere. For example, the News on Japan website colorfully noted in mid-September 2009 that a particularly bizarre dress being previewed for the Spring 2010 Fashion Week in New York was "inspired by a Yoko Ono brainfart." It's even part of several domain names: you can download the Brain Fart game onto your iPhone; tune into Brainfartradio.com; read film reviews at Atomicbrainfart.com; and thrill to that most awe-inspiring, downright shocking example of all, the . . . the . . . uh, er . . . *Brainfart!*

44

SUBTERRANEAN FARTSICK BLUES

A toothless termite walks into a bar and asks, "Is the bar tender here?"

You know what's funny about that joke? There's no such thing as a toothless termite. And if one ever showed up, he'd starve to death, because termites have to work for their supper—and the job *is* their supper. Night and day they're eating whatever wood is handy and gustily expelling its byproducts with gusts of gas that are so teensy weensy you couldn't feel or smell them, and yet those micro-poots ultimately become mighty winds because there are so many termites, countless zillions of them, farting in concert. Back in 1982, scientists from the National Center for Atmospheric Research estimated in a *Science* magazine article that termite flatulence contributed up to 30 percent of the methane in the earth's atmosphere.

"Termites eat a lot of roughage, so they have a huge gas problem," said Terry Clark—who runs Clark Pest Control in Lodi, California—in a conversation with *New York Times* writer Teresa Riordan in 2003. "If you ate wood, you'd have that problem too." And that, says Clark, is the termite's weakness. Its Achilles rear end, you might say.

Termites are so stealthy that by the time you realize they're eating you out of house and home, the damage is already done. So Clark designed his own proprietary methane monitoring system (US Patent No. 6,526,692;

March 4, 2003), which searches for early termite infestation and then kills them before they get near the house.

Here's how he does it. Like a general defending a compound, he sets a perimeter of sentries called Term-Alerts around the house at intervals of ten or fifteen feet. Each one is a two-inch stake (called a "cellulose structure" in Clark's patent), with a four-inch-diameter green plastic disc on top. Pushed into the ground, it looks like a big thumbtack and casts a circular shadow that tells your average heat-sensitive, subterranean termite he's standing under a tree. To a termite, any tree is his life's passion, his life's work, unless he finds a house first. But this time he happens to find what he thinks is a tree. So he goes to work on Terry Clark's stake, which is made of the same Douglas fir that's common in California homes. There's also a little cardboard collar around it—according to Clark, "Cardboard is the junk food of termites." So you can imagine how this termite is practically peeing on himself with joy at finding this stake, not realizing that if he and his pals had kept going another few feet (which must be like a mile to a termite), they'd have a mortgage-free roof over their heads and a lifetime of feasting, flatulence, and fornication—in other words, heaven on earth.

The stake, it turns out, is part of a chamber that leads up to a collection pocket in the plastic lid that traps termite gas. About once a month, a company rep comes around to read the meter, so to speak. He carries a little methane sensor that's not part of Clark's patent. He goes around to each Term-Alert and plugs this sensor into a hole in the plastic lid, and if there's methane inside, the sensor beeps. At that point, the rep pokes a hypodermic-needle-looking thing into the hole and injects a slow-acting poison that gets termites terminally drunk, and they go reeling back into their colony like little Typhoid Marys to share it with everyone.

All because their farts gave them away.

Clark's Term-Alert isn't 100 percent perfect. It can't tell you whether the little pocket of methane inside actually came from something rotting in the soil. But in 2009 his operation is thriving as the largest family pest control company in the country, whose slogan—"Clark, We Need You!"—is familiar to everyone in the Stockton-Lodi region. He and his brother have also expanded the operation and gone green in everything from solar-heating their factory to dispatching vermin with herbs and spices. It's a new day for Clark's Pest Control, and it all started with a simple method of sniffing out termite flatulence. "I was able to patent putting a stake in the ground," he proudly told the *Stockton Record*'s Bruce Spence. "I was amazed that nobody else got there first."

45

EVERYBODY'S FARTING ON YOUTUBE!

Put the word *fart* into YouTube's search slot and you'll get over a hundred thousand hits. Considering that the website was launched only five years ago, in late 2005, that's a lot of videos of people and animals cutting the cheese. You could start watching them now and never get through them in your lifetime. There are folks lighting farts, farting at each other, farting *on* each other, farting in public, farting to interrupt orderly proceedings (like council meetings), farting during auditions for *American Idol*, farting to prove that pretty girls fart, farting in just about any situation you can imagine—and then uploading the results onto YouTube. The animal kingdom is also well represented, from frisky pets to desultory zoo exhibits to creatures of the wild. The democracy of a realm like YouTube gives anyone with a camera and a computer a worldwide venue and proves that we humans are so intrigued by flatulence that we're willing to share it with everyone.

The biggest subgenre within YouTube's farting universe is the over-dubbed video showing a famous person—from Hillary Clinton and President Obama to, well, name your favorite politician or authority figure (the more pompous and self-righteous, the better)—appearing to crack off without compunction or control. These rear-vent ventriloquisms have gotten so popular that already one comedy TV show, CBS's *Late, Late Night with Craig Ferguson*, is airing them. For example, on the morning of June 18, 2009, Ferguson showed a "fart-enhanced" clip of Nevada U.S. Senator John Ensign admitting to the press that he'd had an affair with one of his aides. A week later, June 25, Ferguson ran South Carolina governor Mark Sanford's apology speech for shipping off to Argentina to see his mistress, accompanied by a fusillade of hind-end hisses.

The inspiration for all those videos, the *Birth of a Nation* of faux-farting flicks, is an underground movie called *Pastor Gas*, skewering a real-life Dallas, Texas, televangelist named Robert Tilton, the star of the *Success-N-Life* "prosperity gospel" infomercials that ran throughout the 1980s on over 230 U.S. stations. Tilton's message was that the only way viewers could rid themselves of sin and poverty (one and the same, according to his theology) was to send him a $1,000 "vow" to support his ministry and invest in a personal miracle that would come due sometime in the future; his more secular message was that nobody ever went broke underestimating the intelligence of the American sucker born every minute. ABC News' *Primetime Live* exposed Tilton as a con man in 1991, putting him temporarily out of business, but like most disgraced Southern Gothic evangelists, he was able to find salvation on cable TV. In 2008 he switched his operation to the Internet, where you can find him hawking his books, including *How to Pay Your Bills Supernaturally*.

In 1985 two American prankster-entrepreneurs who have chosen to remain anonymous compiled a number of prime *Success-N-Life* clips and overdubbed all sorts of farting noises to match Tilton's distinctive tics and squints whenever he was lost in the throes of preaching the gospel and "demon-blasting"—that is, shouting prayers at some poor sinning bastard. They circulated VHS cassette copies in the late 1980s under the name *Pastor Gas*. Other distributors bootlegged it under such titles as *The Joyful Noise* and *The Farting Preacher*. After morning zoo radio personalities played the audio over the air, the movie took off and became one of the Internet's early viral videos. Other videos using more recent footage of Tilton began to appear, and an industry was born. These days you can find *Pastor Gas* on YouTube and countless other websites.

Pastor Gas even inspired a 1997 episode of ABC-TV's *The Drew Carey Show* in which Carey made an industrial video to impress his bosses. His coworkers undermined him by secretly overdubbing a squeak or a squib every time he lifted his leg or bent over.

If there's any justice here, it is that the Reverend Tilton will never make a blessed cent from *Pastor Gas* and that he'll spend eternity grimacing in torment, squeezing out the same ungodly farts over and over, like some sad, ridiculous figure in one of Dante's nine circles of Hell.

46

MORE TO LOVE, MORE TO FART!

Here's a big surprise: the Centers for Disease Control and Prevention recently reported that two out of three Americans are overweight and one out of three is obese. If that weren't bad enough, here's an even bigger surprise: a medical journal claims that overweight people eat more, walk less, and require more fuel to get them from point A to point B. They also fart more, and that puts added stress on the environment.

Writing in a 2009 issue of the *International Journal of Epidemiology*, Drs. Phil Edwards and Ian Roberts of the London School of Hygiene and Tropical Medicine said that developed countries with high rates of obesity create up to a billion extra tons of greenhouse gas emissions each year, compared with Third World countries with leaner populations, and that things will only get worse, because obesity is still on the rise in many nations.

"World-wide, over 1 billion adults are overweight and around 300 million are obese . . . [and] there is some evidence that the entire population distribution of [body mass index, the method for determining a person's appropriate weight] may be shifting upwards," the doctors wrote.

But here's the zinger. "Compared with the normal population, the overweight population requires 19 percent more food energy for its total energy expenditure." The doctors broke it down into basic Newtonian physics. "The reluctance of mass to start moving is known as inertia. Energy is required in order to overcome inertia and the greater the mass the more energy is required." That means that people who are overweight have to eat more simply to "maintain basal metabolic rate," even when they're sleeping. At that point, a post-Newtonian law kicks in: eat more, fart more; eat lots more, fart lots more. If big cars are gas guzzlers, big people are gas gushers. Granted, these extra discharges by the heavyweights among us are fairly inconsequential when you consider the other pressures they tend to put on the environment (higher food production, greater use of fossil-fuel-burning transportation, and so on), but still, all that extra pollution blasting from a billion-plus jumbo booties adds up after a while.

Even the Urban Dictionary is piling on, defining "4 kinds of farting fatties," including "*gas giant*: a grossly obese [person] who revolves around food and is comprised of a lot of methane," and "*beefer*: a person who is fat, socially awkward, extremely nonathletic, and permanently smells like a mixture of body odor and farts." It also defines "fart ass" as "when a fat girl wears tight pants but only the ass hangs down so it looks like there is a clump of shit in her pants."

Given today's political hubbub over the threat of cow-fart levies, it's only a matter of time before a few Congressional liberals suggest ways of taxing overweight people's greenhouse gas emissions and conservatives answer by scorning the idea as a Democratic anti-capitalist conspiracy. More ominously, large people could become scapegoats for society's environmental woes. Blogger T-Rex raised the issue in his response to Edwards and Roberts's article: "Did Nazis blaming the Jews for Germany's economic problems in the 1930s start like this?"

Big folks certainly don't need any more grief. They already suffer from high rates of diabetes, heart disease, and respiratory ailments; life's daily routines require much more effort; airlines charge them for two seats; and legions of thin people hate them and think they're stupid and ugly. They're one of the last minorities that people can still ridicule with impunity. And now you've got two scientists claiming that their extra fuel requirements and the attendant "gassing off" are going to tip civilization over the edge. In other words, it'll all be over when the fat lady farts.

On that note, if my high school Latin isn't too rusty, let me say that as far as this book is concerned, "*Obesa cantavit*"—"The fat lady has sung." So I guess it *is* over.

Okay, what have we learned? That farts happen, farts are funny, farts are sometimes famous, and farts matter. They're always leaving us like some angry lover, and yet like buses or streetcars, there's always another one due any moment. They're with us even after we die (briefly, anyway). We can shun them, scorn them, deny them, and stuff a cork up our butts (for a while, anyway, until our heads start bumping the ceiling), but ultimately we can never outrun them. It's best just to embrace them and graciously tell each one, "You're my favorite fart."

So I propose a toast . . . with a Duck Fart cocktail. There are many recipes, but here's the Webtender.com version: Layer, bottom to top, 3/4 ounce of Kahlua, 3/4 ounce Bailey's Irish Cream, and 3/4 ounce Canadian whisky (Canadian Club). Then slam!

Here's to farts. God bless them, every one.

RESOURCES LIST

Aldrin, Buzz. *Magnificent Desolation*. New York: Harmony Books, 2009.

Alper, Josh. "Passing Gas Is a No-No on the PGA Tour." NBCNewYork.com, August 3, 2009.

Anderson, Holly S. "Middle School Issues Ban on 'Intentional' Farting." *Knox County Times* (Maine), February 1, 2008.

Anderson, John. "Women (Real and Fictional) Defying Expectations." *New York Times*, August 20, 2008.

"Anna Friel: I Farted on the Set of Will Ferrell Movie." NowMagazine.co.uk, February 11, 2009.

"Apple's Flatulence Problem." SportsRumorMill.com, July 7, 2009.

"Asafoetida—Uses and Benefits." Online Health Care, 2005.

Atkinson, Brooks. "'Can-Can' from Old Montmartre." *New York Times*, May 17, 1953.

Auerbach, Brad. *"Can-Can." Entertainment Today*, July 19, 2007.

Bagley, Nancy. "Verbatim with Lloyd Grove." *Washington Life*, September 2001.

Balasubramanian, P. "The Smelliest Spice in the World." *The Hindu*, July 30, 2009.

Balderrama, Anthony. "Six Examples of Workplace Rudeness." CareerBuilder.com, March 24, 2009.

Barkow, Robert, ed. *The Merck Manual of Diagnosis and Therapy*. West Point, PA, 1992.

Barrett, Connell. "The Unfunny Life of David Feherty." *Golf*, January 16, 2007.

Beaman, Major Ardern Hume. *The Squadroon*. London: William Cloves & Sons, 1920.

Bedard, Paul. "Animal House in the West Wing." *U.S. News & World Report*, August 20, 2006.

Bennett, Dashiell. "Fart-Gate Officially the Dumbest Sports 'Scandal' of the Year." Deadspin.com, August 4, 2009.

———. "Tiger Woods, David Feherty, Soiled Underpants, and You." Deadspin.com, August 5, 2009.

Berardinelli, James. "The Royal Tenenbaums." ReelViews.com, December 21, 2001.

Billington, Michael. *State of the Nation*. London: Faber and Faber, 2007.

Blitz, Michael, and Louise Krasniewicz. *Johnny Depp: A Biography*. Santa Barbara, CA: Greenwood Publishing, 2007.

"*Blow* (2001)." "Johnny Depp's Farty Humor." InternetMovieDatabase.com.

Bower, Crai S. *Farts—A Spotter's Guide*. Illustrations by Travis Millard. New York: Chronicle Books, 2008.

Bragg, Melvyn. *The Soldier's Return*. London: Hodder and Stoughton, 1999.

Brody, Mike. "Tiger Woods Fart: Real or Fake?" MyFox National, August 4, 2009.

Brown, Mark. "One Man's Laughing Gas Becomes One Woman's Stink Bomb." *Chicago Sun-Times*, December 5, 2006.

Brownfield, Paul. "Sugar, Spice, Everything Not So Nice." *Los Angeles Times*, February 4, 2007.

Budding, Janine. "Hetluchtop.nl, Website for Flatulence, a Hoax." MedicalFacts.nl, August 28, 2009.

————. "Tros Radar Equation Is Wrong: Advertising on Self-Care Resources Is Not Equal to Sign Advertising." MedicalFacts.nl, August 31, 2009.

Cahill, Dan. "Here's the Scoop on Tiger's Toot." *Chicago Sun-Times*, August 6, 2009.

Caro, Marc. "Harold Ramis Confirms 'Ghostbusters III'." *Chicago Tribune*, September 5, 2008.

Carr, William. *Craven Dialect*. London: Hurst, Robinson and Co., 1824.

Carroll, Larry. "Seth Rogen Dissects His High-Minded 'Funny People' Jokes." VH1.com, July 20, 2009.

Caxton, William, *The Cronicles of England*. St. Albans, England: Unknown, 1480.

Chambliss, John. "Gassed Out: Lakeland Kid Kicked off Bus for Flatulence." *The Lakeland Ledger* (Florida), March 19, 2009.

Chartier, David. "Prior Fart: Legal Stink-Up Over iPhone Flatulence App." ArsTechnica.com, February 16, 2009.

"Chavez: 'Bush Devil'; U.S. 'On the Way Down'." CNN.com, September 21, 2006.

Collins, Michael. *Carrying the Fire*. New York: Farrar, Straus and Giroux, 1974.

"Congressman Warns of 'Cow Fart' Tax Causing Beef and Dairy to 'Disappear' from Supermarkets." ClimateRealists.com, June 4, 2009.

Conover, Rodney Lee. "Ten Questions for Sarah Silverman." SportsHollywood.com, 1999.

Conrad, Harold. *Dear Muffo: Thirty-five Years in the Fast Lane*. Briarcliff Manor, NY: Stein & Day, 1982.

Cook, Kevin. "Playboy Interview: Johnny Depp." *Playboy*, January 1996.

Cox, Trevor. "Sounds Funny." SoundsFunny.com, 2009.

Dali, Salvador. *Diary of a Genius*. Trans. Richard Howard. New York: Prentice Hall Press, 1965.

Dana, Bill. *Jose Jimenez—The Astronaut (The First Man in Space)*. Kapp Records LP-1238, 1961.

Daniels, Marques. "Brain Fart Trivia Brings Fun to the Lookout Every Wednesday Night." *San Francisco Examiner*, September 3, 2009.

Darwin, Charles, with Frederick Burkhardt, Duncan M. Porter, et al. *The Correspondence of Charles Darwin, Vols. 10 and 14*. Cambridge, England: Cambridge Press, 1997, 2004.

Daum, Meghan. "The Day the Talk Died at KLSX." *Los Angeles Times*, March 1, 2009, p. A19.

Davies, Caroline. "Search for Britain's Most Remarkable Epitaph." *Daily Telegraph*, April 19, 2008.

Dean, Nick. "Man Stabbed After Passing Gas." *The Lariat* (Baylor University), April 9, 2009.

Dell Pellegrino, Anthony. "Congress, Global Warming and Cow Flatulence." *New Jersey Voices*, June 10, 2009.

D'Estries, Michael Andre. "Alicia Silverstone's Dogs Go Vegan, Lose the Flatulence." Ecorazzi.com, June 24, 2008.

DeWeese, Adrianne. "City Theatre of Independence Puts on Production." *Independence* (Missouri) *Examiner*, September 7, 2009.

Dixon, Robyn. "South Africa Abuzz Over Talk of Banning Soccer Fans' Favorite Horn." *Los Angeles Times*, June 28, 2009.

Dodero, Camille. "Sarah Silverman YouTube Festival." *Village Voice*, January 23, 2007.

Dunne, John Gregory. *Regards: The Selected Nonfiction of John Gregory Dunne*. New York: DeCapo Press, 2005.

"Eco-Friendly Kangaroo Farts Could Help Global Warming: Scientists." *Agence France Presse*, December 5, 2007.

Edwards, Phil, and Ian Roberts. "Population Adiposity and Climate Change." *International Journal of Epidemiology*, April 19, 2009.

Eichele, Tom, et al. "Prediction of Human Errors by Maladaptive Changes in Event-Related Brain Networks." Proceedings of the National Academy of Sciences of the United States of America, 2008.

"Elephants Die of Flatulence." *Bangkok Post*, October 11, 2007.

Elley, Derek. "Thunderpants." *Variety*, May 23, 2002.

Evans, Jennifer. "Consumer Group Catches Media with Fart Joke." *Expatica News*, September 1, 2009.

Fando, Earl. "Footy Notes." UnfortunateIdeas.blogspot.com, June 18, 2009.

"Fashion for Function: The Totally Wacky Wearable Fart Silencer." InventorSpot.com, September 18, 2009.

Felperin, Leslie. "Dublin's Colin Farrell Is Famous for His Big, Filthy Mouth." *Independent*, March 21, 2003.

Flannery, Tim. "Dry Storeroom No. 1: The Secret Life of the Natural History Museum, by Richard Fortey." *New York Review of Books*, December 1, 2008.

"Flatulence Allegedly Sparks Jail Fight." Yahoo! News, December 27, 2006.

"Flatulence Causes Big Stink in Jail." WorldNetDaily.com, December 26, 2006.

Fleming, Michael. "Jonas Bros. Whiff Fox's Farting Dog." *Variety*, October 28, 2008.

"Foul Smelling Felon." *Copenhagen Post*, March 26, 2009.

Francis, Keith. *Charles Darwin and the Origin of Species*. Santa Barbara, CA: Greenwood Press, 2006.

Frank, Justin A., MD. *Bush on the Couch: Inside the Mind of the President*. New York: HarperCollins Books, 2004.

Fuller, Harry. "Fat People an Environmental Issue Now? How about Flatulence?" ZDNet, April 20, 2009.

Galbraith, Kate. "Farmers Panic About a 'Cow Tax.'" *New York Times*, December 1, 2008.

Gardinier, Jeff, "Q&A with Billy Joel." *Details*, August 2008.

German, Bill. *Under Their Thumb: How a Nice Boy from Brooklyn Got Mixed Up with the Rolling Stones (and Lived to Tell About It)*. New York: Villard Books, 2009.

German, Jeff. "'Girls Gone Wild' Producer Ordered to Pay Wynn Millions." *Las Vegas Sun*, August 14, 2009.

"*G.I. Jane* (1997)." "Memorable Quotes." InternetMovieDatabase.com.

Golding, William. *Rites of Passage*. New York: Farrar, Straus and Giroux, 1980.

Googe, Barnaby. *Heresbach's Foure Bookes of Husbandry*. Unknown, 1577.

Graham, Frank. "Felonious Flatulence Leads to Criminal Assault Charges for Jail Inmate." *North Platte Bulletin*, December 28, 2006.

Graham, Mark. "After All These Years, Debra Winger Still Can't Stand Shirley MacLaine's Guts." Defamer.com, January 9, 2008.

Grove, Lloyd, and Elisa Lipsky-Karasz. "Bush Family Laugh Riot." *New York Daily News*, September 29, 2003.

Gunther, Shea. "Boehner Thinks Cow Farts Are Funny." NewsNetwork.com, April 21, 2009.

Hall, Justin. "Just for Laughs, Day 6." *The Independent*, July 28, 2009.

Hansen, Leif. "Penis Burned by a Fart." *B. T. Nyheder*, April 12, 2002.

Harder, Ben. "Fart Like a Kangaroo (and Save the Climate, Too)." *U.S. News & World Report*, January 4, 2008.

Harland, David M. *The First Men on the Moon.* Chichester, UK: Springer-Praxis Publishing, 2007.

Harvey, Steve. "The Chili's Gone But a Few Bowls Remain." *Los Angeles Times*, August 2, 2009.

Hawkins, W. Royce and John F. Zieglschmid. "Clinical Aspects of Crew Health," *Biomedical Results of Apollo*. Washington, DC: NASA Headquarters, 1975.

"Hello, Dolly!" TurnerClassicMovies.com, 2009.

Hernandez, Ernio. "Cole Porter Musical Can-Can—with New Book—Opens in Pasadena." *Playbill*, July 7, 2007.

Hippocrates. *The Full Text of Hippocrates, Vol. 2.* Trans. W.H.S. Jones. London: William Heinemann, 1923.

Hitchcock, Laura. *"Can-Can*/A CurtainUp Los Angeles Review." *CurtainUp*, June 2007.

Hodgins, Paul. *"Can-Can." Orange County Register*, July 8, 2007.

Holder, Travis Michael. *"Can-Can."* Entertainment Today, July 12, 2007.

Holiday, Pete. "Middle School Bans 'Intentional' Flatulence." USLaw.com, February 5, 2008.

"If Pigs Could Fly." *San Francisco Chronicle*. April 11, 1995.

"iPhone Flatulence Fakers Feud." FoxNews.com, February 18, 2009.

Jahnke, James. "CBS's David Feherty, Not Tiger Woods, Was Fairway Farter at Buick Open." *Detroit Free Press*, August 5, 2009.

Jameson, Marni. "Diets? Not for Them." *Los Angles Times*, October 12, 2009.

Jha, Alok. "Carbon Emissions Fueled by High Rates of Obesity." *Guardian*, April 20, 2009.

"John Boehner Cites Cow Farts as Justification for His Environmental Negligence," PoliticsDaily .com, April 20, 2009.

Jones, Kenneth. "Daniels' 'Escanaba' Is a Real Gas." *Detroit News*, October 12, 1995.

Joseph, John. "World's Oldest Joke Traced Back to 1900 B.C." Reuters.com, July 31, 2008.

Joyce, James. *Ulysses.* Oxford: Oxford University Press, 1998.

Kelley, Kitty. *The Family: The Real Story of the Bush Dynasty.* New York: Doubleday, 2004.

Kim, Ryan. "There's an App for All Kinds of Inane Things." *San Francisco Chronicle*, July 10, 2009.

Kirby, Mark. "Megan Fox Was a Teenage Lesbian." *GQ*, October 2008.

Klemmer, Pauline. "The Six Muslims and US Airways." TheStarliteCafe.com, November 21, 2006.

Knaus, Robert. "Secrets of the Furious 5." DVDinMyPants.com, November 9, 2008.

Kotzwinkle, William, and Glenn Murray. *Walter the Farting Dog.* Berkeley: Frog, 2001.

Kovac, Marc. "Senate Resolution Says Fee for Animal Emissions Stinks." *Youngstown Vindicator*, May 7, 2009.

Krull, Kathleen, and Paul Brewer. *Fartiste: An Explosively Funny, Mostly True Story*, illustrated by Boris Kulikov. New York: Simon & Schuster, 2008.

Lazar, Carol. "Downwind of a Farting Elephant." Independent Online/IOLTravel.com.za, July 29, 2004.

Levick, Barbara. *Claudius.* New Haven: Yale University Press, 1993.

Lipinsky, David. "The Unsinkable Kate Winslet." *Rolling Stone*, March 1998.

MacBride, Stuart. "I Am Bin Away, and Stuff." Halfhead.blogspot.com. August 19, 2008.

Malkin, Marc. "John Mayer: 'Twitter Is Silly and Dumb.'" E! Online, March 27, 2009.

"Man Causing Real Stink in Waco Motel Room Gets Stabbed!" Associated Press, April 8, 2009.

"Man Charged After Allegedly Farting Toward Cop." *Los Angeles Times*, September 25, 2008.

Markey, Sean. "New Weapon Against Warming: 'Flatulence Cards' Offset Dog, Human Emissions." *National Geographic News*, March 6, 2007.

Marohasy, Jennifer. "Pardoning Jenny Cracknell's Flatulence." Jennifermarohasy.com, February 17, 2007.

McNulty, Charles. "Here's a 'Can-Can' That Can Deliver Kicks." *Los Angeles Times*, July 9, 2007.

McNulty, Edward. "Coming-of-Age Film Opens." Presbyterian News Service, August 31, 2009.

Menhinnit, Dan. "There's an Ad Offer in the Wind." *The Sun*, September 3, 2009.

Miller, Greg. "If a Boss Farts in a Demo, Should You Engage Him or Run Away?" AskMen.com, May 28, 2009.

Modine, Austin. "IBM Tries to Patent Teleconference Sound Effects." *Register*, September 18, 2009.

Montaigne, Michel de. *The Complete Essays*. Trans. M.A. Screech. London: Penguin Classics, 1993.

Montgomery, Rick. "The 'Keister Bomb' Is the Newest Terror Threat." *Kansas City Star*, September 29, 2009.

Moore, Matthew. "Funniest Whoopee Cushion Sounds 'Long and Whiny.'" *Daily Telegraph*, March 12, 2009.

Morris, Steven Leigh. "The Power of the Fart." *L.A. Weekly*, January 6–11, 2007.

"Mr. Khrushchev Goes to Washington." NPR: On the Media, July 10, 2009.

Musto, Michael. "Sarah Silverman Is My Kind of Cunt." *Village Voice*, January 16, 2007.

Ndola. "Not About the Soccer." Blogs.IOL.co.za/InsideIOL, June 23, 2009.

Noah, Timothy. "Turd Blossom Must Go." Slate.com, July 11, 2005.

———. "Bush's Fart Joke Legacy." Slate.com, October 2, 2006.

Norman, Tony. "Characters' Emotions Give Depth to Animated 'Mononoke'." *Pittsburgh Post-Gazette*, November 24, 1999.

North, Anna. "Pflbthhhhh!" Jezebel.com, February 19, 2009.

"Norway's Moose Population in Trouble for Belching." Spiegel Online International, August 21, 2007.

O'Neill, Molly. "Cows in Trouble." *New York Times*, May 6, 1990.

Overington, Caroline. "Green Answer Is Blowing in the Wind." *The Australian*, February 17, 2007.

Oxford English Dictionary (Compact Edition). New York: Oxford University Press, 1971.

Page, Lewis. "Suicide Bum-Blast Bombing Startles Saudi Prince." *The Register*, September 21, 2009.

Partridge, Eric, and Paul Beale. *A Dictionary of Slang and Unconventional English*. Hoboken: Wiley, 1998.

Patterson, Troy. "Queen of Farts Lost in the Shallows of The Sarah Silverman Program." *Slate.com*, February 1, 2007.

Pepper, Frank S. *20th Century Anecdotes*. London: Sphere Books, 1990.

Pericoli, Matteo. "In Damnation of . . . Horses by Patti Smith." Vassifer.blogs.com, July 20, 2005.

"Eddystone Light." *Peter, Paul and Mommy, Too*. Warner Bros., 1993.

Petronius Arbiter. *Satyricon*. Trans. Patrick Gerard Walsh. New York: Oxford University Press, 1997.

Picket, Kerry. "Gillibrand Maintains Anti-tax Stance for Farms on EPA Proposal." *The Washington Times*, June 12, 2009.

Pliny the Elder. *Natural History.* Trans. H. Rackham. Cambridge, MA: Harvard University Press, 1938.

Pols, Mary. "Where the Wild Things Are: Sendak with Sensitivity." Time.com, October 14, 2009.

Popik, Barry. "Turd Blossom." BarryPopik.com, August 13, 2007.

Prewitt, Alex, and Jerry Potter. "On Tiger Clip From Buick Open, Another Type of Outburst." *USA Today,* August 3, 2009.

Putnam, Dustin. "Review: Zack and Miri Make a Porno." TheMovieBoy.com, October 24, 2008.

Pyle, Rod. *Destination Moon: The Apollo Missions in the Astronauts' Own Words.* New York: Smithsonian Books/Collins, 2005.

Rabelais, Francois. *Gargantua and Pantagruel.* Trans. John M. Cohen. Franklin Center, PA: The Franklin Library, 1982.

Reinger, Jay. "Can-Can at the Pasadena Playhouse." *The Hollywood Reporter,* July 9, 2007.

Reyes, Robert Paul. "Breaking Wind: Farting Banned By Middle School." AmericanChronicle.com, February 4, 2008.

Reynolds, Matthew. "Rodrigo Upset by Sophie's Wind." DigitalSpy.com, July 28, 2009.

Riordan, Teresa. "Using Termite Flatulence Against Them." *New York Times,* May 12, 2003.

Roosevelt, Margot. "Under Ice, a Threat Bubbles." *Los Angeles Times,* February 22, 2009.

Sarah Silverman Program, The (Season One), "Batteries." Comedy Central/Paramount, 2007.

Schapiro, Rich. "Shot at Harry Reid, Nancy Pelosi Lands CBS Golf Analyst in Hot Water." *New York Daily News,* May 10, 2009.

Schlussel, Debbie. "The Farting Lady vs. The Flying Imams." DebbieSchlussel.com, December 5, 2006.

Scott, Sir Ian. *A British Tale of Indian and Foreign Service.* London: The Radcliffe Press, 1999.

Scott, Sir Walter. *Lady in the Lake.* New York: Macmillan, 1925.

Sex and the City, "The Drought." HBO, August 16, 1998.

Shaman, William, William J. Collins, and Calvin M. Goodwin. *More EJS: Discography of the Edward J. Smith Collection.* Santa Barbara, CA: Greenwood Press, 1999.

Sheffield, Matthew. "Norwegian Moose Blamed for Global Warming." NewsBusters.org, August 22, 2007.

Shu, Samuel. "Flatulence, Not Turbulence, Forces Plane to Land." *The Tennessean,* December 5, 2006.

Sidoli, Dr. Mara. "Farting as a Defence Against Unspeakable Dread" *Journal of Analytical Psychology,* April 1996.

————. *When the Body Speaks: The Archetypes in the Body.* London: Routledge, 2000.

Small, Judy Jo. *Positive as Sound: Emily Dickinson's Rhyme.* Athens: University of Georgia Press, 1990.

Smith, Chris. "Record Breaking Whoopee Cushion." TheNakedScientists.com, October 2006.

Snider, Eric D. "Rebound." RottenTomatoes.com, July 1, 2005.

"Sophie Wins Big Brother 10." MTV.co.uk, September 4, 2009.

Spence, Bruce. "Termite Finder a Gas." *Stockton Record,* May 4, 2003.

Spines, Christine. "Leader of the Pack." *Premiere,* January 2002.

Stacey, Pat. "Colin Hits Hurdles in Identity Search." *Dublin Herald,* August 1, 2008.

"Stamp Tiki Tour Is Hard Yakka But Bit of a Dag." The New Zealand Post, July 4, 2007, p. 5.

Stanley, Alessandra. "Cruel, Clueless and, for a Change, Female." *New York Times,* February 1, 2007.

Stein, Jeannine. "Obesity Rate Increases in Many States." *Los Angeles Times,* July 6, 2009.

Steiner, Achim. "The Environment in the News." UNEP.org, February 21, 2008.

Stephens, Heidi. "Big Brother 10—Final Night Live Blog." *Guardian*, September 4, 2009.

Stewart, Scott. "AQAP: Paradigm Shifts and Lessons Learned." Stratfor Global Intelligence, September 2, 2009.

Stoever, Liz. "Is Taxing Cow Flatulence the Right Way to Prevent Global Warming?" *St. Louis Post-Dispatch*, June 9, 2009.

Thomas, Mike. "Dirty, Harry: Former Bed-Wetter Sarah Silverman Sings, Swears, Gets Laughs." *Chicago Sun-Times*, November 10, 2005.

———. "Where the Wind Blows." *Chicago Sun-Times*, May 20, 2007.

Thompson, Jody. "Big Brother 10 Spy: Sophie and Kris Insist Their Romance Is Real." *Mirror*, June 29, 2009.

Thunderpants. A Pathe Pictures/Sky Movies presentation, in association with the Film Council, of a Mission Pictures production, in association with CP Medien. Produced by Graham Broadbent, Damian Jones, Pete Hewitt. Directed by Pete Hewitt. Screenplay, Phil Hughes. 2002.

"Tiger Woods's Fart Mystery Solved; David Feherty Cut the Cheese." TotalSportsPro.com, August 5, 2009.

Tomas, Amelia. "The Stink in Farts Controls Blood Pressure." LiveScience.com, October 23, 2008.

Topel, Fred. "Dennis Quaid Raises 'Yours, Mine and Ours'." Madblast.com, April 13, 2006.

Twain, Mark. "Some Thoughts on the Science of Onanism." Twainquotes.com.

"User Comments for *The Sarah Silverman Program*." Apps.Metacritic.com, 2007.

Wadowski, Heather. "'The Princess Diaries'—A Film Fit For Royalty." Suite101.com, August 17, 2001.

Walter Anthony, Katey. "Methane: The Sleeping Giant Awakes." *Scientific American*, July 2009.

Walter, Katey M., M. Edwards, G. Grosse, S. A. Zimov, and F. Stuart Chapin III. "Thermokarst Lakes as a Source of Atmospheric CH_4 During the Last Deglaciation." *Science*, No. 318, 2007.

Wetzel, Donald. *The Fart Book*. Watertown, MA: Ivory Tower, 1994.

Wightman, Catriona. "No One Will Take Me Seriously." Digital Spy, August 26, 2009.

Wilson, George R., and Melanie J. Edwards. "Native Wildlife on Rangelands to Minimize Methane and Produce Lower-Emission Meat: Kangaroos Versus Livestock." *Conservation Letters*, July 15, 2008, pp. 119–128.

Wilson, James Q. and George L. Kelling. "Broken Windows." *Atlantic Monthly*, March 1982.

Wood, Beci. "Katy Is Perry Gassy on Stage." TheSun.co.uk, March 17, 2009.

Woods, W. David. *How Apollo Flew to the Moon*. Chichester, UK: Springer-Praxis Books, 2008.

Woodward, Bob. *State of Denial*. New York: Simon & Schuster, 2006.

Wyatt, Edward. "A Sitcom That's All About Me, Sarah." *New York Times*, January 31, 2007.

"Yoko Ono Brainfart Fashion." News on Japan.com, September 19, 2009.

Zehme, Bill. "Cameron Diaz Loves You." *Esquire*, March 1, 2002.

Zimmerman, P. R., et al. "Termites: A Potentially Large Source of Atmospheric Methane, Carbon Dioxide, and Molecular Hydrogen." *Science*, November 5, 1982.

INDEX

Sniff out MORE fartlore FROM JIM DAWSON!

Eminent fartologist Jim Dawson blows the lid off traditional history to reveal the lingering effects of farting through the ages. From dinosaurs to robot dogs, Shakespeare to the Pentagon, these first two books in Dawson's fart trilogy will have you gasping for air.

WHO CUT THE CHEESE? A CULTURAL HISTORY OF THE FART
$9.99 (Canada: $12.99)
978-1-58008-011-8

BLAME IT ON THE DOG: A MODERN HISTORY OF THE FART
$9.95 (Canada: $12.95)
978-1-58008-751-3

Available from TEN SPEED PRESS wherever books are sold.

TEN SPEED PRESS
Berkeley
www.crownpublishing.com
www.tenspeed.com